WHO DECIDES?
by Paul Tyler

with extracts from
Committees: How They Work and How to Work Them
by Edgar Anstey
and drawings by Norman Thelwell

ARTHUR H. STOCKWELL LTD
Torrs Park, Ilfracombe, Devon, EX34 8BA
Established 1898
www.ahstockwell.co.uk

British Library Cataloguing-in-Publication Data.
A catalogue record for this book is available
from the British Library.

ISBN 978-0-7223-4374-6
Printed in Great Britain by
Arthur H. Stockwell Ltd
Torrs Park   Ilfracombe
Devon EX34 8BA

TABLE OF CONTENTS

'The only thing necessary for the triumph of evil is that good men do nothing' – *attributed to Edmund Burke.*

For Nicky, without whose amazing patience my participation in much of what follows could not have happened.

FOREWORD: DR EDGAR ANSTEY

I first came to know Edgar Anstey in the late 1980s, when I renewed my direct campaigning activity in Cornwall, first for an unsuccessful bid to represent the county in the European Parliament and then during an eventually successful attempt to win the North Cornwall constituency. In 1992 – as the recently retired president of the local Liberal Democrats – he rejoiced in the record swing which elected me as their MP.

He became a constant friend, shrewd mentor and staunch if sometimes critical adviser.

However, it was only in 2009, after his death aged ninety-two, that I fully appreciated the full scope of his professional career and personal talents. His extraordinary role in defusing the 1962 Cuban Missile Crisis had only been hinted at in conversations with colleagues, until I read the account in Professor Peter Hennessy's *The Secret State* (2002). As senior principal psychologist in the Ministry of Defence from 1958 he had worked with the chief of the defence staff, Lord Mountbatten, and the chief scientific adviser, Sir Solly Zuckerman, to examine the risks of nuclear war. His leading role in the Joint Inter-Services Group for the Study of All-Out Warfare (JIGSAW) happened to take him to Washington in October 1962, just when the crisis came to a head.

Hennessy reported Anstey's analysis that in the event of a nuclear attack 'there is little point in saving people from immediate death without securing the means of keeping them, and the nation, alive during the following months. The US agencies have not yet accepted the doctrine that breakdown could occur in the US . . . but the exchange of views with Jigsaw has resulted in their devoting some attention to the likely consequences of deliveries of some hundreds of megaton weapons, whereas previously their studies had been confined solely to the effects of many thousands of deliveries.'

This seems to have been a typically modest summary. In meetings with President Kennedy's key advisers, Anstey apparently spoke passionately about the certain dangers of escalation, and the need for negotiation and conciliation, rather than pre-emptive attack. His advice may well have been crucial, in changing the US administration's course and averting disaster.

There was but brief reference to this momentous role at his memorial service, in which I participated. It was the many other facets of his character which caught my attention. His touching love poems sent to his wife-to-be, Zoe, were unexpected, as was his distinguished army career in the Second World War. And the books he wrote during his civil-service career were previously unknown to me, although I recognised his characteristic mix of serious psychological analysis and management expertise with gentle humour and common sense.

One title caught my eye: *Committees: How They Work and How to Work Them*. Since I had been toying with a similar idea – necessarily much less professionally or scientifically anchored, but stimulated by experience of decision-making in a wide variety of institutions, from a Parochial Church Council through to the House of Lords – I speedily tracked down a battered ex-library copy.

The bonus I then discovered was that Edgar had somehow enlisted Norman Thelwell to illustrate his theme. How they came to collaborate nobody seems to know. Their paths may have crossed in Cornwall. Thelwell spent several frustrating years in the 1970s (recorded in *A Millstone Round My Neck*) rebuilding an old Cornish watermill on the River Lyner, just below the house which was about to be our family home for thirty-five years. Indeed, I think I was his local MP for a very few months in 1974.

The result is this book. Egged on by Edgar's family, to whom the rights to his book have reverted, I have dared to match examples of his professional wisdom with more extensive and recent practical examples drawn from my much more dilettantish career.

I hope that the combination may be of use – or consolation – to any reader faced with the apparently intractable challenge of extracting from a group a logical, sensible and practicable decision.

THE AGENDA

Edgar Anstey writes:

Three separate criteria were studied, namely Satisfaction of members with the meeting, Productivity of the group and Amount of residual disagreement after the meeting, and it was found that:

(1)   members tended to feel more satisfaction if the group had a definite structure and followed formal rules of procedure, and if members did not feel that they had to assert themselves to receive a fair hearing. Whether members participated to an equal extent did not affect their degree of satisfaction, so long as each member felt that he had the opportunity to say what he wanted.

(2)   groups tended to get through more items of business if they felt that the problems discussed were urgent, if they knew they had authority to deal with these problems themselves, and if they tackled them in an orderly and systematic manner.

(3)   residual disagreement was greater when there were differences of opinion as to goals, when individual members felt their prestige demanded that their own points of view be accepted, and if there was a feeling of inadequate power to deal with the problems discussed.

. . . . The relative importance of the three criteria would

probably differ in different circumstances. For example, when dealing with a series of relatively superficial items, formality of procedure would make for speed and satisfaction, which in this case would be true measures of efficiency.

Committees, pp.37–8

An important duty is to issue the agenda for the next meeting, having fixed the number of items and the order in which they should be taken. . . . Especially with a Standing Committee, at least half of the meeting is liable to be taken up with reading the minutes of the last meeting and discussing matters arising therefrom, with the result that later items on the agenda are either rushed or not reached.

Committees, pp.82–3

When I was elected Britain's youngest county councillor in a shock election result in 1964 (well, it shocked me) I found myself appointed to the Devon and Exeter Watch Committee. It sounded like a ceremonial assembly, depicted in a Rembrandt masterpiece. In fact, it comprised a large group of councillors and magistrates, responsible for the local constabulary.

With a number of other recently graduated Liberal friends I had visited almost every household in the scattered villages, hamlets and even remote farms around the South Devon town of Ashburton, from Widecombe-in-the-Moor to my then home in Broadhempston. Our canvass call at some of these had been completely unexpected and certainly unprecedented. So too was my victory. I had no idea what I had let myself in for.

Aged twenty-two, and completely ignorant of its work, I prepared carefully for the first Watch Committee meeting. Two items on the agenda stood out: the budget for the following year and the report on manpower from the Chief Constable. Desperate not to be shown up as a passenger with nothing to contribute, the preceding evening I used my limited experience of working in an architect's office to identify that new police-station building costs were running at twice the level per square foot of our projects.

On the day of the meeting I was suitably impressed by the obvious experience and longevity of the members around the table. Three-piece tweed suits dominated, even amongst the few women. After a leisurely start at 11.30 – Devon is a big county – we soon passed through the apologies and minutes, and arrived at the budget. The finance officer gave the briefest of introductions, referring members to many pages of figures and notes. Dead silence. No comments or questions. The numbers of noughts in the schedules were clearly too daunting, too removed from the everyday experience of these decision-makers. I plucked up courage to ask about building costs. Deaf councillors asked their neighbours who this was, having previously assumed that anyone so young must be a junior staff member. The chairman suggested that "Mr Taylor" should speak to the County Architect after the meeting.

Ten minutes into the meeting we moved on to the next item on the agenda, which had hitherto seemed insubstantial to me: should the committee be authorising the breeding of bloodhounds or of Alsatians to pursue escaped convicts from Dartmoor Prison (then a regular occurrence)? All the other members awoke from their reverie and contributed eloquently and at length to this debate. There were heated exchanges as to whether dogs or bitches were likely to be proved most reliable, and whether the latter could be trusted to follow a scent when on heat. Confronted by such expertise I kept quiet.

At 12.45 we adjourned for a three-course lunch (Devon expects travel to meetings to be time-consuming and appetite-inducing). Informal discussion continued throughout lunch. At 2.30 we reconvened and the merits of the two breeds were argued extensively, with copious anecdote and illustration, until 3.45.

With the tea break imminent the chairman wisely summed up the difference of opinion by suggesting that both had their advantages and that we should promote the breeding of both.

After tea, a few stragglers stayed with me to hear the Chief

Constable express his regret that the number of uniformed officers was so far below target strength.

Some years later, I asked the Clerk to the Council, who had been presiding with owl-like detachment at this meeting, if he had fixed the agenda to distract members with dog breeding to avoid careful scrutiny of the budget and manpower issues.

"What do you mean, Mr Tyler?" he said, and then, lowering his voice, "What do you think we clerks are for?"

He clearly recalled the lessons of *Parkinson's Law*. The good Professor C. Northcote Parkinson pointed out that many decision-makers cannot get their minds around big issues, and big financial commitments, way beyond their daily experience, and are only too easily lured into extensive discussion of more familiar minutiae. In his example – item 9 on the agenda, £10 million for an atomic reactor, and item 10, a staff bicycle shed, costing £350 – the former takes just over two minutes of the committee's time while the latter occupies three-quarters of an hour.

He who fixes the agenda can almost always fix the outcome.

THE CHAIRMAN

Edgar Anstey writes:

Opinions differ as to the part that the Chairman should play at meetings of this kind. According to one school of thought he can make his most effective contribution if he acts as group 'leader'. One argument is that by virtue of his position he is likely to be particularly well placed as regards obtaining information relevant to items to be discussed and so, provided he does his 'homework' before the meeting, he should know more about the subject matter than most, perhaps all, other members of the committee. It is therefore reasonable and desirable that the Chairman should form a provisional view on each item before the meeting. Unless the pros and cons are so delicately balanced that he feels quite undecided, he should be prepared to give a lead in what he considers the right direction, though he should not press his view unduly if the majority of the committee urge against it.

In practice, one disadvantage of this conception of the Chairman's role is that in the effort to give a definite lead the Chairman is liable to talk too much himself. He may forget that the purpose of setting up a committee is to draw upon the collective experience and wisdom of members and use the meeting as a sounding board for his own opinions. For example, the Chairman of a recent high-powered committee was a practised and accomplished speaker, who from the outset did most of the talking. This prompted another member of the committee to keep notes over a period. He found that the

Chairman was speaking eighty per cent of the time when the committee were having private discussions, and sixty per cent of the time when they were supposed to be hearing the views of outsiders. Three members of the committee were so irritated that they threatened to resign . . .

Another Chairman, who was the head of an organization, had a special technique which must have disconcerted new members of his committees. His custom, when taking each new item of importance on the agenda, was to gaze at a committee member, summarize what he understood to be that individual's views on the topic and then ask if he had made a fair statement. After repeating this process with each member in turn, he would give his own views on the topic and finally sum up on behalf of the meeting. This particular Chairman's knowledge both of the subject matter for discussion and of the individuals was so great that the other members were seldom able to criticize his statement of what he believed to be their views, or to suggest improvements on his summing up. Nevertheless, this technique is not recommended for general adoption.

Committees, pp.53–4

The role of the chairman in any gathering is both crucial and controversial. After my early experience of council and committee deliberation I experienced the extremes of effective group steerage in several very different regimes.

Of all the presidents of the Royal Institute of British Architects with whom I worked Sir Peter Shepheard was undoubtedly the most adroit chairman. A truly delightful draughtsman, who could sketch with all the delicacy of his contemporary, the more famous architect/artist Sir Hugh Casson, he had a foolproof method for ignoring unwanted contributors to a RIBA council or committee debate. As the meeting progressed, out would come his sketch pad and for the next hour or so he would draw with meticulous attention, avoiding the eye of potentially disruptive members. He called only those who could be relied upon to be both relevant and succinct.

By the time of his presidency (1969–71) I had risen through the ranks to a relatively senior position, so found myself at his left hand on many such occasions. I have on our study wall a striking back view of a female nude, sympathetically created by Peter – so my note on the back reminds me – during a lively discussion at the Policy & Finance Committee meeting on 20 June 1971.

During the meeting, as the coffee was circulated, various members of the female staff looked over the president's shoulder, wistfully hoping that he was drawing from life. I can reliably report that neither they nor any of the women architects around the table were the models for this cheeky prospect (*see opposite*).

On another occasion the president led a small deputation to see the Minister of Agriculture, Jim Prior, in the hope that better standards of farm building design could be encouraged alongside the government grants.

During the desultory discussion with two senior civil servants and the minister himself, who parried all arguments with talk of economies, Peter drew a wise old owl and a perky parrot. At the end of the meeting, when Jim Prior left, the two bureaucrats hurried round the table to see which of the three of them had been caricatured.

Disappointed by the beautiful birds, they had to be further discouraged by my assurance that the president always insisted that a RIBA staff member retained his sketches. These two accompany the other bird on our study wall.

Some years later, in 1983, when I was elected to chair the National Executive of the Liberal Party, I remembered Peter Shepheard's example. I was parachuted into the role – having never served on this body previously – because (I was told) the incumbent was finding it difficult to control the garrulous and meetings were stretching beyond tolerable limits. Sadly, I had no sketching skills, but I found a way of looking thoughtfully over the heads of potentially long-winded contributors and those who regularly wished to revert to the item before last. I survived the permitted three years in the chair, and we did

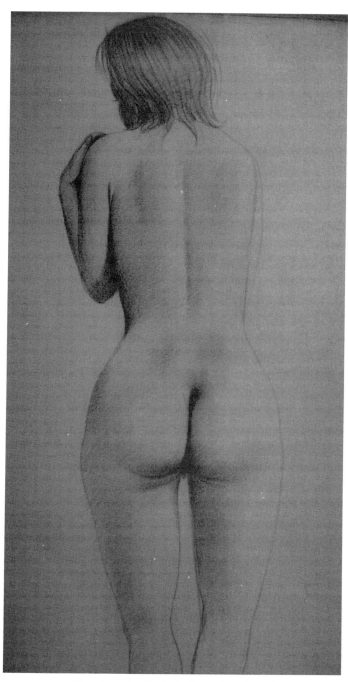

Drawing of a Nude by Peter Shepheard.

manage the agenda of change as the Liberal/SDP Alliance took shape with some semblance of efficiency, and my successors were elected by a rather more democratic process.

The rationale for such a choice can be idiosyncratic. The reason why John Pardoe, former MP for North Cornwall, was chosen to chair the Alliance campaign for the 1987 general election was simple: he was thought by everyone – including both the joint leaders and indeed himself – to be the only person capable and willing to stand up to David Owen and David Steel in equal measure.

I was (and am) a huge fan of John and I confess that I too expected this to work. After weeks of acting as the linkman between the two leaders' campaign tours, and attending the regular meetings of the core team, I knew it was an impossible task. At the final planning meeting, on the Sunday before polling, the agreed line on our attitude to the other two parties in the event of a stalemate – always a media preoccupation even in those days – was to be promulgated by the chairman, John Pardoe.

The two Davids left by different exits from that Whitehall committee room, with distinctly different interpretations of our conclusions for the waiting journalists, and the chairman had to try to combine the incompatible.

John has remained a special friend – and an invaluable supporter in my later bid to succeed him in North Cornwall – but understandably he never wished to engage his talents and amazing energy in national politics again after 1987.

However he or she is propelled into chairing a committee, or indeed any meeting, the chairman can be crucial. The process may be far less significant than the capability of the individual selected.

I have participated in more choices of chairman – or chairperson, but surely never 'chair' – than could conceivably interest you. In a few cases I have been the unexpected and unwitting object of the exercise.

The process can be mysterious. One dark and stormy night, with the hail spitting on the peat fire in a room at Jamaica Inn full of pungent pipe smoke, I was the guest speaker at the annual meeting of the Bodmin Moor Commoners Association. Nominally there only to describe the provisions of a private bill to regularise the management of common land on the moor, which I was promoting with a neighbour MP, I found myself drawn into much more controversial territory. First, in the traditional absence of the honorary treasurer, having innocently sought to explain (in a quiet aside) an apparent double entry in the annual accounts, I was invited to expand my explanation for the whole assembly, alluding to a contra-item. And then, when a totally unheard-of challenge to the normal inheritance of the chair by the vice chairman stunned the meeting, came the inevitable summons: "Mr Tyler – he knows all about elections – how do we do it?"

The lapse into democracy, after a century of nepotistic succession, had clearly unnerved everyone, even the radical element. The tension was palpable, and even the lively debate between the Goodenough cousins about the management of 'entire animals' was stilled.

I decreed a secret ballot, tore up slips of paper myself, and was asked to act as returning officer. After a tense ten minutes of collective contemplation and pencil sucking, I counted the ballot papers and declared the young challenger to be the victor. To the amazement of both the incumbent chairman and the vice chairman, the feudal succession was broken. I was never invited again.

Such antiquated attitudes never (of course) influenced the process by which those who chair the two Houses of Parliament are selected. I have witnessed at close hand elections for both the Speaker of the Commons and the Lord Speaker, and worked closely with both. Although they too 'take the chair' the role is so far removed from that of any other presiding chairman that it deserves special attention. See the next chapter.

A Two-Faced Chairman.

SPEECHLESS SPEAKERS

Edgar Anstey writes:

At meetings governed in the main by an external discipline, the contributions that any individual member can make are limited by set rules enshrined in the constitution or established by the practice of the committee, and interpreted and applied by the Chairman. The rules are designed to facilitate keeping order and to enable sensible decisions to be reached quickly and with least effort. The Chairman has authority to secure that preference is given to those members who can make the most useful contributions, so that committee time is occupied as efficiently as possible. At meetings of this type, the proceedings are usually formal, with precise agenda and limited time for discussion of each item. Any member wishing to speak must catch the Chairman's eye, and it is within the discretion of the Chairman to select the next speaker and to decide when disagreements must be resolved by majority vote. The theory underlying this method of committee meeting is that, even when all the relevant facts have been made known, opinions are liable to differ; that it is not therefore always possible for the committee to reach agreement and prolonging the discussion indefinitely serves no useful purpose; and that after a reasonable amount of time has been allowed for discussion and exchange of views, the best course is to sound the opinion of the meeting (either by a formal vote or by some other device) and then go on to the next item on the agenda. The Chairman controls the proceedings so as to achieve precise objectives.

Committees, p.28

I don't think Edgar Anstey had local or national government particularly in mind, and I am quite certain nobody in the Palace of Westminster has ever seriously attempted to apply his analytical approach to the business of Parliament. Perhaps they should.

The role of the Speaker in the Commons (and his or her deputies) and the Lord Speaker in the Lords (and her or his deputies) would benefit from a review based on his professional advice.

As a relatively insignificant spokesperson for the relatively small group of Liberal MPs in the short 1974 Parliament I had very few contacts with the then Speaker, Selwyn Lloyd. Apart from a successful Privilege Complaint in July – when the Glasgow Chapel of the National Union of Journalists (NUJ) tried to discipline me, as an NUJ member, for voting against relaxation of trade-union legislation – I had little occasion to approach him directly.

However, when I reappeared in the 1990s, after eighteen years in real life and as the prize retread, I gradually became much more involved with the running of the House, and therefore I was in regular touch with the Speaker. In particular, there were innumerable encounters between May 1997 and my retirement as MP in April 2005, when I served as Liberal Democrat Chief Whip and then Shadow Leader of the House, and as a member of the Modernisation and Procedure Select Committees.

Betty Boothroyd was elected the first woman Speaker, to great acclaim, immediately after the 1997 Labour victory. I think it would be fair to say that she was content to accept the role just as it was, with no ambition to lead the House towards any rationalisation of its procedures, but to attach to it her own very special character. As such, she became a household celebrity but did not attempt any modernisation.

No doubt she would say that was not her proper function as Speaker.

And yet she was faced with a clear need for just such rationalisation. The Blair government had arrived with a clear mandate, based on the pre-election Cook–Maclennan agreements, to achieve improvements to the way in which the Commons worked. At the same time the more than double strength of the Liberal Democrats – from twenty MPs in 1992 to forty-six – and the huge majority of Labour over the Conservatives (418 to 165) meant that Parliament had to adjust itself to totally different arithmetic. This was no longer a bipolar assembly of roughly equal numbers, but a tripartite gathering of very unequal dimensions.

And Madam Speaker herself, a veteran of strictly two-party politics, soon found this had practical implications. Newly elected by my colleagues as their Chief Whip, my first priority was to try to find somewhere for us all to sit. Liberal Democrats had hitherto been confined to one bench in the Chamber, behind the natural rebels of the main Opposition party. We needed a 'front bench'.

The severely reduced Parliamentary Conservative Party (cut from 336 to less than half that, their lowest number since 1906) could clearly afford to let us have some of their spare space. However, they resolved to resist to the last when it came to that front bench. I had to mobilise my troops for 6-a.m. picket duty, Wednesday after Wednesday, to place 'prayer cards' along the desired front bench to be able to occupy it for Prime Minister's Questions. Even so, a few equally determined Tories managed to get in there as well. Eventually we had to occupy the main Opposition front bench at the outset of the day's proceedings, to make our point, whereupon a very unseemly row ensued. The Speaker went ballistic and I was summoned to see her afterwards. A visit to her snug was a daunting experience at the best of times, not least because of the severe passive-smoking risk.

However, once I had explained what had been happening, that the official Opposition leadership was apparently quite relaxed about our needs, and that we had offered to retain the corner seat below the gangway for their Father of the House (Ted Heath), she agreed that we were not being unreasonable. The word went out that the Tory mavericks should back off. The Liberal Democrats got their front bench and, seated there beside him, I had the repeated joy of hearing Ted Heath's sotto voce comments about his colleagues.

Nevertheless, the daily operation of the House continued on the assumption that there were only two sides to every question, despite the multiparty representation of the much more diffuse party allegiances of the electorate.

It was just one example of the way in which the Speaker could, and can, exercise huge influence to oil the wheels of the Commons.

With the long-practised advice of her secretary, Nicholas Bevan, Madam Speaker avoided embarrassing challenges in the chamber, usually maintaining order without too frequent interventions. Outside, when Labour Leaders of the House – and especially the more radical Robin Cook – sought to edge procedure into the twenty-first century she put no insuperable obstacles in the way.

Equally, she did nothing to encourage greater accountability in the Members' expenses regime, acquiescing in the repeated failure of successive Prime Ministers to implement independent recommendations to increase MPs' pay while turning a blind eye to their expenses claims. The cumulative result exploded around her successor.

Wisely she decided to retire before the end of the 2001 Parliament, so that the new Speaker could get accustomed to the role before the inevitable changes of membership at the following general election.

Michael Martin's arrival in the chair in 2000 was controversial from the outset. By past convention a Conservative MP (or even a Liberal Democrat) would have been expected to get substantial backing from the Labour side, both to achieve some alternation and to ensure that the Speaker was not thought to be in the government's pocket. Martin was resolutely supported by his Labour colleagues, some claiming that snobbery was the cause of the misgivings for his candidature (he took great pride in his former occupation as a manual boilermaker). Once elected he made a point of hobnobbing with his mates in the Members' Tea Room, which seemed to some to display inverted snobbery.

On my first visit to the Speaker's apartments after he took over Martin proudly showed me how thoroughly his wife had cleansed the kitchen, and driven out all trace of cigarette residue everywhere.

His attempted spring-cleaning of the staffing was less successful. He fell out with Bevan (it was said that he considered the latter's rather dry manner to be a condescending reaction to his own working-class origins) and suffered as a result from less experienced advice in the chamber.

More seriously his failure to recognise the gathering storm over the totally inadequate accountability of the Members' expenses scheme, and his maladroit attempts to fend off media interest and investigation, escalated the problem. His attitude seemed all too reminiscent of an old-style shop steward trying to cover up the sharp practices of his union members.

As credibility slid away so his role in the chair became ever more fraught. It was not so much that Members became more individually unruly. It was more that the whole assembly seemed increasingly rudderless. By the end even his closest friends could not claim that he could *control the proceedings so as to achieve precise objectives*.

At times he seemed incapable of making his voice heard. When a Speaker feels he must speak – and shouts of "Order" have little or no effect – then he or she is fatally wounded.

What damage to the office of Speaker his failings, and his subsequent removal, have caused is hard yet to establish. Mr Speaker Bercow has made valiant efforts to reassert the authority of the chair, while also showing himself much more sympathetic to change, not least in the transparency with which the Commons administers itself.

His election, however, was not without controversy either. Although a Conservative MP, he was broadly backed by Labour and Liberal Democrat Members in a newly agreed secret ballot, precisely because it was thought that this would irritate the Conservative leadership; and, sure enough, his attitudes once elected have done just that.

Again some critics suggest that Bercow speaks too much, intervening too often, and is too free with the witty put-down for his own good.

When the Lords decided on the guidance to be followed by their own Lord Speaker, following the decision to remove the Lord Chancellor from the Woolsack in 2005, the prevailing distaste for the way in which both Madam Speaker Boothroyd and Mr Speaker Martin had become increasingly vocal in the chamber at the other end of the corridor influenced opinion. It was agreed, for example, that the Lord Speaker should have absolutely no active role during Questions: neither then nor during debates would he or she, or any other occupant of the Woolsack, give even a gentle hint regarding who should contribute next. This invidious task was left with the government Chief Whip, or another front-bench spokesperson for the executive. Not only does this seem perverse, when the questioner selected may be more or less sympathetic to the government, but by definition the choice is left with someone who has his or her back to many of those seeking to be chosen.

The first Lord Speaker, Hélène Hayman, may have found this enforced impotency frustrating, but I suspect she found the way in which the Labour and Conservative leaders' and whips' offices carved up the business, through the 'usual channels', even more so. The idea that the House of Lords is 'self-regulated' is an absurd conceit.

When the hustings took place for her successor, the very presence of ex-Speakers Boothroyd and Martin in the Lords was a constant reminder of the perceived need to avoid the pitfalls of the Commons experience.

The successful candidate for the Lord Speakership, Frances D'Souza, gained support by cleverly quoting the response of Speaker Lentall to King Charles I in January 1642, when he demanded to know the whereabouts of Oliver Cromwell and the other four MP enemies of the Crown: "I have neither eye to see, nor tongue to speak here, but as the House is pleased to direct me, whose servant I am here." She won because the conservative instincts of so many peers reacted against any suggestion of a pro-active occupant of the Woolsack. In fact, the 'usual channels' won yet again.

In both Houses, therefore, those who would welcome a more productive atmosphere would do well to consider carefully Edgar's detailed advice at the head of this chapter. Parliamentary proceedings may be essentially formal, but they otherwise have very little resemblance to the ideal picture he paints.

And the lack of effective chairmanship throughout the Palace of Westminster would seem to be a principal weakness of parliamentary discussions.

Ventilation is Most Important.

DIVINE APPOINTMENT?

Those in the know tell me that the episode in Yes, Prime Minister *in which the appointment of a bishop is described in hilarious, hair-raising detail was remarkably perceptive. I take this to mean that they have witnessed something similar in real life.*

When the objective is to discover the best candidate for the new Archbishop of Canterbury, Primate of all England and leader of the Anglican Communion worldwide, we may assume that the process is even more thorough, but the potential pitfalls even more hazardous.

There are common elements. For example, different Prime Ministers have taken significantly different attitudes. Tony Blair was very hands-on, while Gordon Brown – the self-proclaimed Son of the Manse – was decidedly hands-off. The former took a personal interest in the selection of the chairperson for the commission which eventually recommended Rowan Williams. On another occasion he refused to nominate either of the candidates recommended for a major diocese, and ('rightly', I am advised) insisted on a rerun.

By contrast, Brown backed off even from expressing a preference when offered a couple of equally well-qualified names for a diocesan bishopric. Instead of backing a candidate, he obsessively tinkered with the process. This was generally considered to add unfortunate complication rather than welcome simplification. David Cameron, as in so many other respects, seems to be following Blair rather than Brown, if only because he comes from an Anglican background.

Way back in the nineteenth century these were seen to be very influential appointments in English society, and Queen Victoria herself took a personal interest in many of them. In the twentieth century episcopal 'interference' in politics caused frequent bouts of strained relations and public criticism, not least at the time of the abdication crisis. Yet the process was neither very systematic nor at all transparent until the premiership of James Callaghan, in the 1970s, when a concordat was agreed and the role of the Crown Appointments Commission regularised the process.

Critics believe that all this history has tended to fossilise the appointments process in the Church of England. To the outsider this may seem to be a labyrinth of anomalies and anachronisms. It has, of course, grown up over the centuries. But in the last twenty years or so efforts have been made to systematise the processes and make them better understood by all participants.

There are some 10,000 English parishes, each with a 'patron', often the bishop, but for 700 or so it is the Crown or Lord Chancellor, and No. 10 is nominally responsible. The parish appointments are handled according to diocesan systems. Beyond that level two-thirds of the deans, the sixty suffragan bishops and the diocesan bishops themselves are now appointed through a more rational system. Those who now operate the selection process believe that – in the main – it is well understood in the Church and works far better than it used to.

Of course, that is just England: Wales is disestablished, Scotland has a different Established Church and Northern Ireland is impossible to describe.

The smaller-fry English vacancies would be advertised in the Church Times, *but until very recently this was* thought to be beneath the dignity of more senior appointments. Similarly, interviews have crept in and CVs are more structured, but the common thread has often been personal encouragement or personal acquaintance. The involvement of the representatives of the particular Church community seeking a replacement clearly leads to extensive ferreting around for acceptable candidates.

It can appear to the casual observer very much like the Barchester Chronicles. For those like me, who have actually read and still enjoy Anthony Trollope's novels, it should be remembered that he was describing a Church which was vastly different in wealth, status and social standing from the Church of England of today. For example, the temptation to examine the suitability of episcopal wives was described to me as 'very natural but very naughty'. Twenty-first-century concepts of natural justice, let alone modern legislation, rule that out.

There are obviously considerations. As in other walks of life, what credibility do you give to the enthusiastic endorsement of the candidate's present boss? Is he (not yet usually 'she') just trying to get rid of an awkward subordinate? What overriding attributes are you looking for – leadership, conciliation or crisis management?

This brings us back to the new Archbishop of Canterbury. The selection team was authoritative. Chaired by Lord Luce, a lay Anglican from the heart of the establishment (former politician, Governor of Gibraltar and Lord Chamberlain) they included two bishops, six representatives from the Canterbury diocese, three lay people and three clergy from the General Synod and one primate from the wider Anglican Communion. That last member raises an intriguing question: could a bishop from America, Australia or Africa be chosen? And if they were, how could they qualify to sit in the House of Lords? Would they have to acquire British citizenship?

On previous occasions the then Archbishop of York was a member of the commission, but this time round John

Sentamu did not want to be ruled out as a candidate – and the Bishop of London also opted out for the same reason.

In late September 2012, when the commission process accelerated, the bookmaker Paddy Power put the odds on the declared episcopal runners as follows: Stephen Cottrell (Chelmsford), 25:1; Nick Baines (Bradford), 20:1; John Inge (Worcester), 20:1; Richard Chartres (London), 9:1; James Jones (Liverpool), 11:2; Justin Welby (Durham), 9:2; John Sentamu (York), 7:2; Christopher Cocksworth (Coventry), 15:8; and Graham James (Norwich), favourite, 13:8.

I happen to know Bishop James best, since he was the suffragan bishop in Cornwall during part of my time there as a local MP, and he has contributed effectively in the Lords. But how the bookies measured up this lot is even more of a mystery than the prayerful deliberations of the commission itself.

The process of shortlisting took months, culminating in three days of interviews. The elusive search for balance clearly preoccupied them. With an outgoing 'High Church' archbishop (was he really?) should they go for an 'evangelical'? Or if Sentamu was to remain at York, should they redress the balance in the other direction with the appointment of a traditionalist? And if they plumped for him, what did that do for balance at the top of the Church?

The superbly well-informed Andrew Brown, writing in The Guardian on 21 September, admirably summed up the most problematic element in the role of the archbishopric: 'In some very nebulous sense he is also the leader of the Anglican communion, a worldwide body with no agreed doctrine and no discipline, which has rejected all attempts to supply it with either.'[1] In this context it may be surprising that the only non-English contribution to the commission came from a Welshman.

They were required to recommend one name and also

a 'second appointable candidate' to the Prime Minister.

Chairing this process required diplomacy, patience, perhaps some divine inspiration . . . and probably also a blind eye to the bookies' favourites and the prejudices of the pundits. Dame Elizabeth Butler-Sloss (as she then was), the very senior judge who chaired the 2002 Commission, was thought to have been exemplary in this role, but the verdict must always depend on the apparent success of the appointee, the new archbishop himself.

As a decision-making process for the twenty-first century, in a so-called mature democracy, this may all seem curiously introvert and irrelevant. But the proof of this pudding lies in the eating: will the eventual product prove to be to the taste of the Church and the nation?

With the accession of Justin Welby, the general reaction of the media and the people in the pews seems to be "So far so good." Does that justify this rather convoluted process?

1   A. Brown, 'Five Jobs at Once but Little Power: The Race to Be Archbishop Is On' in *The Guardian*, 21 September 2012.

THE SECRETARY

Edgar Anstey quotes:

> And so while the great ones depart to their dinner
> The secretary stays, growing thinner and thinner
> Racking his brain to record and report
> What he thinks that they think that they ought to have thought.

and comments:

> . . . in preparing minutes or a report, the Secretary has to exercise, not only skill in drafting, but also judgement.
>
> For example: (1) Committees often reach conclusions by irrational means, out of mistaken loyalty, or in pique, or exasperation. If so, the Secretary has to endeavour to rationalize their views or, if this proves impossible, to give them a chance to alter their conclusion. (2) In order to keep the minutes or report reasonably concise, the Secretary has to exercise discretion as to what to put in or leave out.

> *Committees, pp.84–5*

He who records a decision is more powerful than they who make it. I don't actually know whether someone else has already suggested this, but, however cynical, there is some truth in it.

The role of the scribe who manages and records the decision-making process – whether in a village WI or the House of Commons – can be as influential as it is secretive.

Indeed the two commonly used words 'secretary' and 'secret' have related Latin origins.

My most instructive time as a secretary was in 1981/2, when David Steel asked me to take on this task for a Liberal/SDP Alliance commission on employment. My only qualification for the job was that I was currently out of work. Five years running a local newspaper group in Cornwall had come to an amicable conclusion, following the company's takeover by a national media giant.

I was scarcely prepared for this challenge, but the members of the commission certainly made up for my ignorance. The idea was that the Alliance needed to give some intellectual weight to its policy development, hitherto a rather hit-and-miss concoction of such policy instincts and personal hobby horses as the leaderships of the two parties happened to share. The hope was that this would create a semblance of a joint election platform, to underpin the run of by-election successes already achieved and prepare the ground for the anticipated general election in 1983.

To fulfil this ambition the two leaders (David Steel and Roy Jenkins) persuaded a galaxy of talent to serve on the commission. In addition to some heavyweight politicians (John Pardoe, Nancy Seear, Bill Rodgers, Richard Wainwright, Shirley Williams and Ian Wrigglesworth) they recruited three formidable intellects from other fields. Aubrey Jones had recently retired as chairman of the Prices & Incomes Board, Richard Layard was then Professor of Economics at the LSE and a hitherto little-known Professor of Investment from the University of Birmingham called Mervyn King all contributed some notable expertise.

This future Governor of the Bank of England was only an occasional contributor, and I don't recall being particularly impressed. Layard, however, simply fizzed with ideas and – better still – with thoughtful contributions for my then very sketchy report. Some arrived from distant parts of the world. He was later to give much needed advice to the Gorbachev regime in Moscow, as part of perestroika, steering sceptical economists and administrators towards more realistic economic management. He has ended up – like me – in the House of Lords, but sits on the Labour benches and has achieved renewed fame as the authentic guru on happiness.

The secretarial lessons I learnt were legion. First, never attempt to compress divergent views into a false consensus. Secondly, never suppose that your own views have any significance in such company. Thirdly, however much the chairman (in this case a distinguished industrialist) may insist on his pre-eminence, don't let him take over your own role as chief draftsman. Fourthly, beware of those whose skill is to blind with science rather than illuminate for those of limited intellectual sight. Finally, always remember that any mistakes or misunderstandings that your report is thought to have committed will be entirely your fault, while its wit and wisdom will be entirely due to the skill of the committee members.

The title of our 1982 report was *Back to Work*. And that was exactly the advice I took. After several weeks' campaigning as the Alliance candidate in the Beaconsfield by-election – where we had the satisfaction of pushing the Labour nominee (one Anthony Charles Lynton Blair) into a deposit-losing third place – I was headhunted to lead a public-affairs consultancy team.

This experience was probably untypical. The clerks in both Houses of Parliament, for example, steer their committees with extraordinary tact and diplomacy, given that they invariably know far more about the matter in hand than the bunch of amateurs with which they are saddled. Since the party whips normally choose the membership for their ignorance and their reluctance to rock boats with unwelcome expertise, the clerks have both huge opportunities and huge problems in producing coherent reports, let alone legislation which is capable of practical implementation. By contrast, my commission was landed with a relative ignoramus. I moved on as soon as I could, before I was found out.

I am not sure how many of our recommendations reached the real decision-makers, but at least one more real job resulted – mine!

COMMITTEE MEMBERS

Edgar Anstey gives this advice on tactics to committee members:

(1) Master the papers beforehand, preferably not too long beforehand. Look up any relevant facts from the original source or as near to it as possible, and be prepared to quote both the facts and the source (e.g. the relevant section of an Act, or the relevant paragraph of a book or report) in support of your argument.

(2) When the time and place of a meeting are being considered, try to stick to your home ground, while being accommodating about date and time of day.

(3) Make your guests comfortable and offer hospitality to make them feel friendly disposed towards you. Do not overdo the hospitality, however, to such an extent that your guests will agree to things which they will later regret.

(4) If you are disagreeing with another member, build your argument on some point he has made. Do not be obvious and say 'But you yourself said . . . .', but be more subtle and include your opponent's form of words in your own statement. This will seem to him familiar and perhaps more acceptable.

(5) It sometimes pays to flatter, though here again the references should be oblique and not too obvious.

(6) At a meeting, be prepared to go on as long as is necessary to gain your point, letting the other side get exhausted first.

(7)   If an opponent has a bad argument, let him talk about it as much as he likes, so that you will have more weak points to demolish.

(8)   Take advantage of likely exhaustion, and introduce the topic on which you particularly want agreement when people are too tired to argue but have just enough time to consider it before they disperse to catch trains, etc.

(9)   Never overstate your case. When opposition is likely, spike your opponent's guns by conceding his main points (these can with advantage be overstated slightly, so that he is forced to withdraw somewhat in order to avoid looking ridiculous) but suggesting (not necessarily stating) that there are counters to them. If possible, keep one argument in reserve, to produce with telling effect when apparent deadlock has been reached.

(10)   It sometimes pays to say 'to be frank . . . .' Or 'speaking bluntly . . . .', while remaining as polite as possible. This may induce the other side to place **their** cards on the table.

(11)   If the difficulties are practical, stress the point of principle. If they are theoretical, stress that you are a practical man.

(12)   Where a compromise seems inevitable, start from an extreme position, so that you have maximum room for manoeuvre.

(13)   Concede nothing until you have to and then make full play with the fact you have made a concession and expect one in return.

If you are supporting the weakest party in a three-cornered vote, the best chance of success is to induce the two bigger parties to vote against each other first. Then if neither party wins a majority, your proposition or your candidate may eventually be adopted faute de mieux.

Committees, pp.77–9

This is where Edgar Anstey puts his finger on the most critical advice for anyone involved in committees or other collective decision-making.

He rightly concentrates on the appropriate characteristics for effective committee membership. He gives the impression that it is possible to select the best possible mix, rather than (as is surely much more often the case) having to make do with what you are landed with.

However, it is surely rare for the chairman – or indeed anyone else actually deputed to suffer from the result – to have a free hand in selecting the membership of a committee. Even the party whips in the Commons and Lords have to meet all sorts of competing claims and objections when appointing to select, bill or joint committees. Collusion and cooperation can go so far, but not far enough to guarantee gender balance, or broad representation of views, let alone a harmonious mix.

When I first surveyed the Liberal Party National Executive from its chair in 1983 it was just such a muddled human menagerie. Apart from a few ex officio members, whose attendance was as erratic as it was useful when they did show up, the majority were elected by a variety of routes and methods. Some clearly won their place by sheer determination, with such staying power elsewhere in the party's nether regions that nobody else had the resilience to challenge them. Others were the residue when the more active members in their region or affiliated body had all decided to be active campaigners locally, rather than devote their weekends to boring London meetings. Others again were filled with naïve ambition to steer the party to national victory: they usually failed to contribute after a few meetings and drifted back to their constituencies before the end of their term to become much more effective as councillors.

As Liberal Democrat Chief Whip I attended the Tuesday afternoon meetings of the Committee of Selection, when we each put forward the names from our respective ranks for that week's nominations to parliamentary committees. On one occasion, when the regular chairman was absent, as the longest-serving MP present I chaired a meeting which made several such appointments in less than one minute.

That elective dictatorship has been replaced now by some democratic internal election of select-committee members in the Commons, but the resultant mix is scarcely better balanced. And membership of the committees which actually decide on the content of legislation is still carefully managed.

Two particularly dysfunctional categories of committee member seem to be especially prevalent: 'minute men' and 'delayed reactors', in this as in so many other organisations. The former save up their challenges to the accuracy of the minutes of the previous meeting, and meticulously comb through these at the beginning of every session. Often of marginal significance, betraying the fact that the discussion and decision had escaped the member concerned, they can take up an inordinate amount of valuable time. I have known up to half the planned meeting being distracted by a couple of such minute men.

Worst of all, these individuals will sometimes leave the meeting early, if only to be able at the next meeting to misunderstand the minutes all over again.

Delayed reactors dominate the other end of a committee meeting, with their afterthoughts. Just as the long-suffering survivors of earlier items are shuffling their papers for an unobtrusive exit, and the chairman is about to draw the discussion to a close, these overanxious members are determined to raise points under 'Any Other Business'.

Typically, these relate to one of three types of issues: first, an issue that was discussed and decided at a previous meeting which the member did not attend; secondly, an issue which was determined earlier in that meeting when there was a fuller attendance, but which the member calculates could now go a different way; and, thirdly, an issue which is so irrelevant to the whole agenda that the only way the member can climb on his or her hobby horse is to bring it up in this way and at this juncture.

My mentors long ago recommended the best way to deal with both minute men and delayed reactors was to adjust the agenda subtly: against the item 'Minutes of Previous Meeting' the words should be added 'Comments and corrections are to be submitted to the secretary seven days in advance of the committee meeting'; and the final item should read 'Any Other **_Relevant_** Business'.

By these means I hoped to slim down the meetings of the Liberal Party National Executive, and we did indeed have some success, but my memory is that I left the chair after three years (to assist with general-election planning) with regrets of unfinished business.

My other experiences of chairmanship have revealed huge variations in the extent to which different members bring commitment, application and imagination to committee work.

One almost universal characteristic stands out: we are all likely to respond more positively, and with better recall, to visual images than to the spoken word.

I can give two classic examples. Chairing a committee on 'The Future of the Village' in the mid-1970s for the then Council for the Protection of Rural England I steered discussion with limited success, given the excess of enthusiasm and expertise around the table. Few concepts secured general concentration for any length of time before one member or another gathered us all up on to his or her favourite hobby horse – until, that is, our gifted young architect produced drawings of acceptable and unacceptable design elements for residential buildings in his home county of Essex. We all lapped up his strictures. To this day I can see the impact of the narrow top-hung window he had condemned as the 'deadly night light'.

My other example is taken from a presentation my team and I made to the Countryside Commission, when my public-affairs consultancy was seeking to raise its profile with a wide range of target audiences. Having painstakingly analysed weaknesses, strengths and opportunities, and suggested new messages and methods of communication, the slide show turned to a modernised house style. Up to that point there had been relatively little audience reaction. Our team anticipated disappointment. However, once my always imaginative colleague, Judy Craddock, head of our design team, took the floor the commissioners all snapped to attention. She illustrated the themes of our recommended change of emphasis with her usual panache. In particular, she produced a delightful new version of the commission masthead with two letters in the word 'Countryside' subtly suggesting an adult holding a child's hand to cross a stile. For nearly an hour individual commissioners debated whether this would encourage *too many* people to seek more access to the countryside, provoking landowners who were already apprehensive of any new demand of the right to roam, thus undermining the commission's attempts to build consensus between the extremes of rambler aspiration and crop protection. This new logo was not adopted.

Long before computerised communication media became commonplace, committee members recognised a simple message when they saw one.

A Mixed Committee.

SELECTION AND ELECTION

Edgar Anstey writes:

In the field of selection, a Board is sometimes summoned ostensibly to select the best from a short list of candidates: in reality the appointment has already been decided, and the Board does no more than confirm a decision already taken. To the extent that the members of the committee are aware of the position, they are likely to feel resentful that they are being used as rubber stamps.

Committees, p.11

The desirability or otherwise of prior consultation or 'lobbying' before a meeting is a point of particular interest. . . . One's attitude to the ethics of prior consultation is likely to depend very much on the circumstances and on the phraseology used to describe the form of consultation. Inviting another committee member out to lunch, for instance, can be described as showing 'desire to explore in a relaxed situation the full implication of items to be discussed' or in less flattering terms. On the whole, one might say that the process of getting together beforehand to discuss the issues and reach preliminary agreement, as described in C. P. Snow's *The Masters*, is either a very good sign (if the aim is simply to save time) or a very bad sign (indicating feuds).

Committees, pp.74–5

In three-quarters of British constituencies, at times an even higher proportion, the Member of Parliament is in effect selected by his or her party. In these 'safe seats', it is cynically observed, a baboon with the right colour rosette would always win. That makes a local party or association's selection contests vitally important.

I am pleased to say that the three major parties have each tightened up their processes since my time, both to promote gender balance and diversity in the outcome of their selections and to ensure the resulting candidature does not cause reputational damage. Following several high-profile MEP and councillor selection calamities, even UKIP may have learnt the same lessons.

Yet no matter how many rules are instituted to govern the process of a selection, human instincts and interactions still inevitably shape its outcome. Anstey's analysis of selection boards – and my practical experience of them, albeit at a more relaxed, even eccentric, period in our politics – will still ring many bells with those involved today.

My first selection for a Cornish constituency in 1968 was instructive. Although it was then held by the mercurial, even melodramatic, Liberal MP Peter Bessell it was far from a safe seat. His majority in 1966 had been a fraction over 2,000 votes.

As a county councillor in neighbouring Devon, with an unremarkable but respectable result in the previous general election in Totnes, I was placed on the longlist. Bessell told me he had personally recommended my name to the Bodmin Association chairman; I subsequently discovered that he told several of the other candidates the same thing.

We were summoned to meet the selection committee, who would prepare a shortlist for a general meeting of all the Liberal members. This encounter took place in the office of a prominent Liberal accountant in Plymouth, over the Tamar (and therefore over the Cornish border into Devon) to ensure no leakage to the prying journalism of the editor of the *Cornish Times*.

I don't know how my competitors got on, but my interrogation was somewhat idiosyncratic. My views on the independent nuclear deterrent (sceptic) and the European Common Market (very sceptic) were only briefly considered. Most of the forty minutes of exchanges concentrated on my mother's ancestry: my direct descent from Bishop Jonathan Trelawny, coupled with the arrival of ancestors in St Kew in 1066 and my grandfather's ministry in at least three of the parishes in the constituency, appeared to carry much more weight than any policy preferences.

At the time I was bemused by this emphasis. My siblings and I had enjoyed our family history, but we never seriously entertained the thought that Mother's ancestry had any great significance, let alone potential career advantage. The Bishop is a Cornish folk hero, since he was one of the seven to challenge James II in 1688. He was arrested and tried for 'seditious libel', and his acquittal by a London jury in Westminster Hall triggered the Glorious Revolution that brought William and Mary to the throne. James described Trelawny as "the most saucy of them all", an epitaph I myself fancy. Whenever a group of Cornishmen and Cornishwomen gather together they are liable to break into the 'national' song: "Shall Trelawny live or shall Trelawny die, here's twenty thousand Cornishmen shall know the reason why."

Subsequently I learnt that the discussion after my interview had been more concerned with my Anglican membership than my political views. Allegiance to a party in Cornwall was then largely determined by denominational difference. One of my predecessors, visiting the committee room in the fishing village of Polperro on polling day, asked the local Liberal chairman, the builder and undertaker, how things were going.

"Very well, Mr Roseveare" came the reply.

Stuart was nonplussed: in the 1950s Liberals did not do well, even in Cornwall.

"How do you know, Mr Libby," he said.

"Well, this year we'm buried ten of they and only six of ours, Mr Roseveare."

A funeral service in the parish church meant a Tory decease and one in the Methodist chapel a Liberal one. Labour did not feature in rural Cornwall.

Even in my own time some of this tradition prevailed. My close Liberal colleague and much missed friend David Penhaligon, newly elected MP for Truro in 1974, encountered a mystified supporter in Tregony.

"I'm told you're Church of England," he challenged David.

"That's right."

"And I'm told you're teetotal."

"That's right."

"What's the point of you being teetotal if you be Church of England!"

Later, of course, I got to know all those committee members very well indeed, and realised that their insistence on personal connections – and personal commitment – reflected a shrewd assessment of Cornish electoral priorities.

When it came to the full association meeting, at which the members were to choose from the committee's recommended shortlist, there was still a flavour of the former discussion. For a start, it took place in the Isaac Foot Memorial Hall, with pictures and memorabilia of the great man all around us. Isaac, MP for Bodmin at various times between the two world wars, and founder of the remarkable political dynasty of Foots, was a powerful radical Liberal orator on six days of the week, according to my mother, and an equally devastating preacher from the Methodist pulpit on the seventh.

The other candidate, favoured by the retiring MP, was a London QC with rather more limited Cornish connections. With the previous experience of the committee interrogation in mind I shamelessly explored my ancestry, reminding members that Trelawny too was an Anglican. I won by a reasonable margin, rather more comfortably than when I eventually became MP (after missing out quite badly in 1970) with a majority of just nine votes in February 1974.

If you think that selection process was eccentric, let me tell you it seems positively humdrum compared with that for the Liberal candidate to fight the 1973 parliamentary by-election in the Isle of Ely. This account comes direct from a conversation I had with that candidate – none other than my colleague Clement Freud. It is accompanied by the warning that he was always the most brilliantly entertaining and creative raconteur.

He was on a business trip to New York in the summer of that year when he had a telephone call from Jeremy Thorpe, the then Liberal leader. Would he be interested in becoming an MP? Freud thought it was not quite that simple: didn't one have to be elected? And surely the general election was not to be called for another year or two? Thorpe made it sound so straightforward. The Conservative Member for Ely, Sir Harry Legge-Bourke, had died and there would be a by-election; the Conservative candidate was hoping to inherit his substantial majority, but Ely, said Thorpe, was clearly winnable by the right Liberal candidate, since Sir Harry had taken the seat off the Liberals in 1945. There was likely to be a swift campaign, because the Tory high command would not want to enable a Liberal bandwagon to get under way. He did not mention to Freud that in the previous general election, in 1970, the local Liberal Association had not even been able to contest the constituency.

Freud was intrigued by the invitation and returned from the US to discover that there was indeed a hint that the campaign would be accelerated. What Thorpe had also failed to tell him was that another name had already been suggested by Liberal Headquarters to the local association: a very well-briefed councillor called David Penwarden. The members would choose.

Now, I should remind you that Clement Freud – 'Clay' by nickname to his friends – was at this time regularly appearing in a TV advertisement, seated beside a very doleful bloodhound. If anything, Clay looked even more lugubrious than his co-star, and the joint endeavour had become something of a cult hit.

When the constituency secretary, who was also the matron

of a large old-people's home, heard the two names on the shortlist, she was horrified. There were only eighteen paid-up members – which might explain that failure to contest the seat in 1970 – and she could not bear to expose this weakness to such a national celebrity as Mr Freud. Being very resourceful she told the residents that "the TV Dog Man" was coming to town, and for a very small subscription they could all attend the show.

Less than a week later (this is still Clay's personal account) he and Penwarden addressed the full membership of the association, now swollen to some fifty or so, in the meeting room attached to one of the town's pubs. In the first three rows sat a number of elderly ladies, with a smattering of even older men, the former mostly knitting throughout. David Penwarden spoke first, demonstrating a comprehensive knowledge of Liberal policy. Clay confessed to having only a very sketchy awareness of any policy, but told his audience that the poll could take place very quickly and he would have the advantage of being already well known. He told some amusing stories. The old ladies stopped knitting and applauded.

When the vote was taken almost all the long-standing members supported the policy expert, but Freud had a large majority from those recently recruited from the retirement home.

Within a few short weeks he was back in that very room, after a typically rumbustious and media-friendly campaign, to celebrate his election as MP with a substantial majority he was to increase dramatically at later elections. And a very conscientious, effective and admired MP he was too, as I witnessed myself when I joined him on the Liberal bench in the following year.

My next encounter with a selection committee was in 1982, when David Penhaligon, then our parliamentary by-election supremo, persuaded me to throw my hat in the ring in Beaconsfield. This choice was not especially memorable, since as an ex-MP I had a clear advantage over the local councillor. He was thought to be unlikely to cope with the national media attention, inevitable after the string of Liberal/SDP Alliance by-election victories and near victories.

Much more interesting was the selection-committee experience – and subsequent careers – of the two other party candidates, Tim Smith for the Conservatives and Anthony Charles Lynton Blair for Labour.

The seat had become vacant on the sudden death of the veteran right-winger Sir Ronald Bell at the end of February. The circumstances of his departure were sufficiently lurid to occupy pages of print in *Private Eye*, but very few of the conventional residents of South Buckinghamshire read it.[1]

On paper the constituency was one of the safest Conservative seats in the country, with a majority of 21,495 (41.5%).

The national media, however, were very interested from several points of view: the colourful character of the previous MP and his peccadillos, the recent emergence of the Alliance as a serious challenger to the bipolar nature of English politics and last but not least – as the campaign got under way – the coincidence of the Falklands War.

Tim Smith was up against formidable opposition in securing the Beaconsfield nomination. He had been the surprise victor in a previous by-election at Ashfield in 1977, overturning a Labour majority of nearly 23,000, but he lost it again in the 1979 general election. So he was not that safe a pair of hands.

There were more than 100 applications for the seat, including Sir Ronald's eldest son, Andrew, and two others who were later to become very well-known MPs: Edward Leigh and Bill Cash. After an exhaustive selection-committee process – described to me by one of the then Constituency Association officers as "we knew we could be appointing someone to Parliament for life" – the field was reduced to a manageable shortlist. The hustings ballot approached 400

---

1   By far the most comprehensive and revealing account of this period of Tony Blair's career – and indeed of the cause of the Beaconsfield by-election – is contained in Francis Beckett and David Hencke's *The Blairs and Their Court* (London: Aurum Press, 2004) to which readers are referred for more extensive description and analysis.

votes, but ended with a tie of 184 each for Leigh and Smith. The aristocratic chairman of the meeting, Lord Burnham, used his casting vote to give Smith the nomination.

The contrast with the Labour selection process could not have been more stark. There were only four applications. The Labour leader of the neighbouring council of Slough, John Hurley, apparently performed badly at the only meeting at which the four were questioned. Anthony Blair, smart London lawyer, long-haired and debonair, was later dubbed 'Deb's Delight' in Gerrards Cross, but after his selection was announced the *South Bucks Observer* reported it under the headline 'Benn-backing Barrister is Labour's Choice'. His appeal consisted of a loyal reiteration of Michael Foot's then current policy stance: exit from Europe, ban the bomb and doubts over the military adventure to recapture the Falklands.

Blair had previously sought nomination in Middlesbrough and Stockton with dispiriting lack of success, and his foray into Beaconsfield was said to have resulted from the fact that his wife, Cherie, was proving to be more employable (and therefore earning more) at the Bar than he was. Had this not been so, she might well have taken to the hustings first, and, indeed, in this by-election her political antennae seemed far better tuned than his. However, he clearly learnt quickly the art of political career advancement.

On 27 May, with British troops poised to liberate the Falkland Islanders, Margaret Thatcher appealed for votes to 'support our brave boys' and the Conservative election address sported a large picture of the Tory agent in Second World War battledress. The candidate was far too young to own such garb, but he became the victor nonetheless. I moved the Liberal/SDP up several percentage points into second, pushing Anthony Blair into a deposit-losing third place with a drop of the Labour vote from 10,443 to 3,886. Not exactly the most propitious start to an electioneering career!

His next move was characteristic. He eyed up the fast-approaching general election and identified a new constituency (created after boundary changes) consisting of former mining villages on the fringe of Darlington and Durham. According to later myth-makers he snatched 'the Sedgefield nomination at the last moment, solely by means of his own heroic efforts and those of his five obscure supporters in the little village of Trimdon, led by the ever-loyal Trimdon branch secretary John Burton, all alone against the powerful party machine.'[2]

The reality was rather different. Tony Blair (Anthony was dispensed with in the move from Buckinghamshire to Durham) spent months targeting the two most powerful trade unions in the country, the GMB and the TGWU. He had given some legal advice to the former, so he started with Tom Burlison, its Northern Regional Secretary and formidable fixer of Labour politics in the area. Later he talked to Joe Mills of the TGWU. Leading lights on the right of the party, like Neil Kinnock and Roy Hattersley, determined to stop the candidacy of a Bennite called Les Huckfield, were also deployed to reinforce his credentials. The possible appearance of Tony Benn himself, knowing his then Bristol seat was very vulnerable, made them redouble their efforts.

'The trouble with plotting, when there is a lot of it about, is that the plotters start to fall over each other's feet. In the case of the Sedgefield nomination there were plots and plotters galore,' wrote Beckett and Hencke later.[3]

The Trimdon connection does seem to be genuine. His evening with John Burton – whose widespread connections throughout the area were to compensate for Blair's lack of them for many years – and four other Labour stalwarts secured a vital branch nomination. Most significantly Micky Terrans was impressed. He was the chairman of both the Constituency Labour Party and the local council.

On 18 May 1983, when the general-election campaign was already under way, the executive reduced the sixteen names submitted by local or union branches to six. Blair was not among them.

Next day the much bigger general committee, with 111

2   Beckett and Hencke, *The Blairs and Their Court*, p.61.
3   Beckett and Hencke, *The Blairs and Their Court*, p.63.

delegates, met to approve the shortlist. None of the candidates were allowed to attend. The committee was permitted to add names. John Burton moved that Blair be added: 'I have here a letter from Michael Foot thanking Tony for his performance in the Beaconsfield by-election and stating that he would like to see him in the House of Commons as soon as possible.'[4] After a few further exchanges Terrens put the proposition to the meeting, and it was announced as being carried by 41 to 40. According to Beckett and Hencke that vote was not so clear-cut, and it was challenged by some left-wing union delegates, but Terrens stood firm.

On the following day Blair had to confirm his support for unilateral nuclear disarmament, when each of the seven candidates were questioned, to appease the left-wingers. Meanwhile the TGWU contingent swung into action with awkward questions for his rivals.

After three ballots four of the seven remained. On the fifth, with second and third preferences reallocated, Blair beat Huckfield by 73 to 46 votes.

On Thursday 9 June – less than three weeks later – Tony Blair was elected MP for Sedgefield with a majority of 8,281. I don't suppose he had ever encountered Edgar Anstey, let alone read his little treatise on committees and lobbying, but he had a natural talent for the latter and the various committees he had to deal with in his subsequent meteoric career don't seem to have noticed.

Meanwhile Tim Smith prospered in Parliament, becoming a junior minister and vice chairman of the Conservative Party until he unwisely and inexplicably accepted cash in a brown envelope from the owner of Harrods in exchange for asking a parliamentary question. His career ended on the eve of the 1997 election.

In the last few days of the Blair premiership, Cherie unexpectedly invited Nicky and me for a drink in their private flat in No. 10. She and I had briefly exchanged light-hearted messages recalling the Beaconsfield battleground of twenty-

4   Beckett and Hencke, *The Blairs and Their Court*, p.69.

five years previously. Tony had just had his final audience with the Queen, following the Falklands anniversary ceremony, and he reappeared from the palace to find us on their sofa, covering up his surprise admirably.

I gently pointed out that had he won in Beaconsfield in 1982 he would undoubtedly have lost the seat back to the Tories in the general election a year later. The Labour Party would have been unlikely to offer him another winnable by-election seat in the 1983–7 Parliament, during which others would have risen the steep and slippery slope towards the party's leadership.

Cherie immediately spotted that I was thinking of Gordon Brown and looked at Tony; he broke into a genuinely relaxed grin.

WORKING GROUPS

Edgar Anstey writes:

> Any group of people working together over a period will almost inevitably develop a corporate spirit and desire to conform. Tolerance of differences of opinion within the group is equally desirable and important.

Exeter College academic Chris Ballinger in his *The House of Lords, 1911–2011: A Century of Non-Reform* astutely observes that 'seeking a perfect reform through consensus is a fast-track to inertia'.[1]

In the search for just such a consensus, in February 2003, the House of Commons was given the opportunity to vote on seven options for the reform of the House of Lords, as set out by a joint committee of the two Houses.

I must take my share of the blame for the resulting debacle. Not only was I a member of that joint committee, and was instrumental in urging that all options – from all appointed to all elected – that appeared to have any support should be listed in our report, but I also persuaded Robin Cook, the Leader of the Commons and the minister responsible, that each should be tested to see if we could establish an optimum solution. I confess that I was following my usual dictum: it is usually more productive to ask people to choose between A and B, rather

---

1 C. Ballinger, *The House of Lords, 1911–2011: A Century of Non-Reform* (Oxford: Hart Publishing, 2012), p.218; this is by far the most comprehensive and carefully researched assessment of the whole period of failed attempts at reform.

than between Yes and No, since the latter choice almost always results in the 'don't knows' voting No.

However, I failed to convince Robin that the votes should be preferential, so that we would be guaranteed a convincing result. Understandably, he felt that his Cabinet colleagues – already doubtful about the whole reform agenda – would baulk at anything that looked like a proportional voting system.

So MPs were faced with eight options (not so much a choice between A and B as a choice between everything from A to H): A, total abolition; B, fully appointed; C, fully elected; D, 80% appointed; E, 80% elected; F, 60% appointed; G, 60% elected; and H, 50% each way. On the night they didn't bother with the C, F and H, and narrowly defeated the 80%-elected option (E) by just 284 to 281, but rejected by the largest margin the fully appointed option (B).

Meanwhile – unsurprisingly – the peers voted by three to one for that very solution.

At the end of the evening Robin Cook said, "We should go home and sleep on this interesting position . . . the next stage in the process is for the joint committee to consider the votes in both Houses. Heaven help the members of the committee, because they will need it."

He was right.

Before the committee was able to be established Robin had resigned, on the eve of the US/UK invasion of Iraq, leading the Labour rebels and joining with all the Liberal Democrats and the gallant fifteen Conservative MPs led by Ken Clarke in the opposition lobby. The Cook/Clarke nexus was to prove extremely valuable.

On 9 May the joint committee attempted to pass the whole issue back to the government, effectively washing its hands of any responsibility. Some of us felt that this was excessively defeatist, especially with Robin no longer in charge. So I engineered an unofficial 'minority report', signed by nine committee members, including Ken Clarke and William Hague. We argued that the overwhelming rejection of the fully appointed option by MPs made it 'absurd and unacceptable to introduce legislation which would have that effect'.

For the rest of 2003, when not inevitably obsessed with Iraq, Tony Blair and his colleagues shied away from any progress on this front, instead settling down to a gruelling campaign to remove the law lords to a supreme court, and to abolish the Lord Chancellor as an afterthought.

During 2004, however, I detected that more than twelve months of inaction had created a change of mood on the back benches. This was still unfinished business. I asked Robin Cook and Ken Clarke if they would be prepared to see if we could come up with a draft bill to fulfil the most popular option of the previous year's votes by MPs – a mainly elected second chamber. We recruited two other formidable parliamentarians, Dr Tony Wright and Sir George Young, and set to work with the professional help of Dr Meg Russell of the Constitution Unit at University College London (UCL) and a parliamentary draftsperson.

Meg had previously provided Robin with invaluable advice and assistance, as resident expert on all such reform issues during his period as Leader of the Commons. Her previous academic studies of the Lords – and indeed her monumental 2013 work, *The Contemporary House of Lords*[2] – give no real indication of how she applied her expertise to contemporary politics at that time. Today's cautious academic was then a formidable campaigner.

The discussion of electoral systems was especially instructive. I left it to Robin to explain the advantages of a proportional system to Ken Clarke and George Young, since as a Liberal Democrat I was so clearly compromised by impractical idealism. The clinching argument he used was that first-past-the-post would create locally competing rivals for MPs. The traditional Conservative resistance to PR dissolved.

Our efforts bore fruit with the 2005 report *House of Lords Reform: Breaking the Deadlock*, and a professionally drafted bill, much of whose recommendations have resurfaced in subsequent proposals.

Our cross-party quintet published the report and draft bill on 21 February 2005, supported by some thirty other

2   M. Russell, *The Contemporary House of Lords: Westminster Bicameralism Revived* (Oxford: OUP, 2013).

parliamentarians, from both Houses, who endorsed our general ambition to keep the cause of radical reform alive.

By careful submission to the Speaker we secured a ninety-minute debate in the 'Sitting in Westminster Hall' two days later, brilliantly led by Robin Cook but with contributions from the other four of us. The Hansard report (HC Deb, 23 Feb 2005, col.71 WH) makes interesting reading even now, since all the previously and subsequently troublesome issues seem to have surfaced in the exchanges. Nevertheless there was a hardcore of genuine consensus, which survived remarkably even through the following general-election campaign.

And this experience demonstrates all too clearly the substantial contrast between the broadly based committees described in the bulk of this book and a small group of like-minded individuals who, while representative of different viewpoints, come together with a specific, limited and agreed purpose. We were united in our determination that the apparent deadlock should be broken.

We started with a broad consensus and were therefore able to achieve a unanimous outcome – a rare opportunity indeed.

A similar but inevitably far from identical opportunity for a cross-party initiative to influence government and parliamentary decision-making occurred in 2012.

After lengthy but abortive negotiations on possible constraints on donations to and expenditure by political organisations in the 2005–10 Parliament all three major parties attempted to position themselves on the side of the angels. Their 2010 general-election manifestos promised to 'take the big money out of politics':

> The public are concerned about the influence of money on politics, whether it is from trade unions, individuals, or the lobbying industry. We will seek an agreement on a comprehensive package of reform that will encourage individual donations and include an across-the-board cap on donations. This will mark the end of the big donor era and the problems it has sometimes entailed.
>
> *Conservative manifesto*

We believe that the funding of political parties must be reformed if the public is to regain trust in politics. Our starting point should be the Hayden Phillips proposals of 2008. We will seek to reopen discussions on partyfunding reform, with a clear understanding that any changes should only be made on the basis of crossparty agreement and widespread public support.

Labour manifesto

We will get big money out of politics by capping donations at £10,000 and limiting spending throughout the electoral cycle.

Liberal Democrat manifesto

The May 2010 Coalition Agreement spelt out the intention of Cameron and Clegg to make progress. In 2011, frustrated by lack of action but encouraged quietly by Ministers to review the options, the Committee of Standards in Public Life (CSPL), chaired by Sir Christopher Kelly, got to work on the issue. Their eventual and very thorough report, published in November 2011, set out a gradual programme, anticipated to take some years, for the implementation of both donation caps and limits on campaign spending.

Nick Clegg asked David Laws (then out of ministerial office) to convene a small 'official' group to explore the potential for cross-party agreement: with John Denham (for Labour) and (Lord) Andrew Feldman (for the Conservatives), and representatives for each party headquarters, they spent some twelve months, with a succession of meetings and papers, getting nowhere. At regular intervals I met David – who was scrupulous in maintaining the confidentiality of the process – to discuss ways in which I might help push things along from the outside, but he became increasingly pessimistic about the outcome.

In the summer of 2012, aware of this lack of progress and becoming increasingly concerned at the risk of ever more blatant attempts to buy political influence – the US experience looked ominous – I explored the possibility of some backbench activity, across the three parties, to reinforce the official negotiations. I suppose I hoped for a similar positive initiative to that of seven years previously, and the Joseph Rowntree Reform Trust were also optimistic. We decided to attempt a draft bill, following closely the main recommendations of the CSPL. So far so good.

Finding allies in the Conservative and Labour Parties proved more difficult. A handful of MPs and peers, from each side, seemed natural recruits, but, for a variety of reasons, didn't want to become too closely involved. Some were happy to give advice; some were prepared to express support, but doubted the good faith of everyone else; some were well intentioned, but defeatist; one wanted to undertake a vast public consultation exercise before producing any draft legislation; and one was enthusiastic to help so long as his name was kept off the actual published proposals ("I am already out of favour in No. 10 on so many other issues"!).

An added complication was that Andrew Tyrie, one of the very few Conservative MPs to have given serious thought to these issues over many years, was simultaneously submerged in an exhaustive commission on the banks. He had little time for anything else, although, as he had been a prolific writer in the past, we had some previous contributions to which we could refer. Occasional telephone conversations, while he navigated the route to or from his Chichester constituency, were hardly sufficient once we started work on the project in earnest.

On the Labour side the choice narrowed down to a senior MP who had also studied the issues previously, as a member of a select committee which had undertaken a limited investigation some years earlier: Alan Whitehead proved a reliable and conscientious, if naturally cautious, contributor.

In differing ways the three of us, with Alex Davies (my indefatigable parliamentary assistant), were able to set out the objectives for the drafting of the bill, to be undertaken by a professional, Stephanie Grundy.

We followed faithfully the CSPL recommendations in

almost all particulars. Only in the area of 'non-party' or 'third-party' campaign funding did we feel the need to go further. As I discovered, in my conversations with the Electoral Commission, it was becoming all too evident that the constraints on party donations and expenditure – especially if they became incrementally more effective – would cause displacement into less accountable areas, with potentially huge distortion.

As I later pointed out, when we launched our draft bill, a Russian oligarch or maverick multi-millionaire (bored with buying football clubs) could spend vast sums seeking to influence public opinion in advance of election or referendum campaigns. . . . And the regime determining what the political parties were allowed to do would be virtually powerless.

That launch had to be postponed, since our originally planned date precisely coincided with Margaret Thatcher's funeral, and would have taken place within yards of her resting place off Westminster Hall, before the procession to St Paul's. The delay took us beyond the date of the Queen's Speech, with the advantage that we then knew that all efforts by Nick Clegg, David Laws and other Liberal Democrat ministers to include legislation on this issue (in common with the related issue of lobbying) had come to nothing. In my contribution to the debate on the 'Gracious Speech' I bemoaned this lack of action, and hoped a bill would appear as one of the 'other measures' always added as a footnote to the government's programme.

At a standing-room-only seminar on 16 May, chaired expertly by Sir Christopher Kelly, Alex and I laid out the options, with contributions from a number of prominent Conservative and Labour parliamentarians. However, we had little hope of action. The three parties had retreated into defensive indecision – until the remarkable events of the very last days of May.

That weekend the *Sunday Times* and the BBC *Panorama* programme combined to mount a sting operation. No doubt they failed to fool several other parliamentarians, but they appeared to have trapped Conservative MP Patrick Mercer and a couple of Labour peers into accepting paid lobbying roles for a fictitious Fijian initiative. All of them denied any wrongdoing (advocacy for a fee or retainer is banned by both Houses), but immediately Messrs Cameron and Miliband were vying with each other to demonstrate that they were not responsible for the failure of all cross-party efforts to deal with the distorting influence of big money in our body politic.

We were back in business.

Over the next six weeks we must have had a dozen or so exchanges – meetings and messages – with the ministerial team. At first the lobbying proposals took centre stage, and we thrashed out a careful minimalist approach which concentrated on transparency: who was talking to whom about what and when? This required a parallel improvement in the speedy reporting of relevant meetings with ministers by commercial lobbyists, to match information on their clients. We felt that inclusion of every single organisation, charity, pressure group or constituency representative would merely swamp the system, and make it less navigable or accessible for the public and the media.

Into this already complicated situation dropped another bombshell. Following a well-oiled fracas in the Strangers' Bar the sitting Labour MP for Falkirk was to depart from the Commons, and his safe seat attracted understandable interest. To the horror of the party's leadership Len McCluskey's trade union, Unite, was found to have been on a membership drive there, in an effort to sew up the by-election nomination.

This proved too tempting a target for David Cameron, who accused Ed Miliband of being "too weak to stand up to the Unite union, too weak to run Labour, and certainly too weak to run the country" (HC Deb, 3 July 2013, col.913).

In a speech on 9 July Ed Miliband responded (courageously or craftily, depending on your political viewpoint):

> Our relationship with individual Trade Union members needs to change . . . I do want to change the way individual Trade Unionists are affiliated to the Labour Party through these funds. At the moment, they are often affiliated automatically. I do not want any individual to be paying money to the Labour

Party in affiliation fees unless they have deliberately chosen to do so. Individual Trade Union members should choose to join Labour through the affiliation fee, not be automatically affiliated. In the twenty-first century, it just doesn't make sense for anyone to be affiliated to a political party unless they have chosen to do so.[3]

The result? On 17 July the government introduced its Transparency of Lobbying, Non-Party Campaigning and Trade Union Administration Bill. The bill had been in gestation for some months, of course, but I doubt whether it would have appeared so early, or with such a fanfare, without this series of events. After all, only ten weeks previously the bill had been pointedly omitted from the Queen's Speech.

But from here on the whole issue of 'big money' and politics has been back on the parliamentary agenda.

Who decides? In this case, once again, the answer must surely be "Events, dear boy, events."

---

3   Ed Miliband 'One Nations Politics', transcribed on the Labour website (www.labour.org.uk).

A Homogeneous Committee.

BOOKING A PRIZE

It would be a fair criticism that most of my examples of collective decision-making are taken from the weird world of British politics. It may be that the characteristics Edgar Anstey and I describe are peculiarly evident in this context, but I would submit that they can be found in all forms of public life in this country. In academia, for example, my infrequent but fascinating encounters confirm that they are all too common. And other much publicised examples certainly share at least some of these characteristics.

Some in the literary world, for example, would love to be able to claim that the process by which the annual Man Booker Prize for Fiction is awarded is shrouded in mystery. It helps them justify their annual row over the choice.

As is so often the case, the really intriguing question is 'Who selects the selectors?'

The answer is not especially elusive. Ion Trewin, Literary Director of the prize and a very approachable Cornishman, is far from secretive. His background may be significant. Author of a remarkable biography of the flamboyant Alan Clark, and editor of his equally colourful diaries, Mr Trewin is himself a persuasive figure in the world of books, with much of the credit for the very successful Cheltenham Literary Festival.

He is advised by a hierarchy of wide-ranging

bookworms, from all walks of the reading public, but his choice of five to form the annual 'jury' is rarely challenged. His key criterion would seem to be a passion for books, without any predominant professional interest. The mix, in recent years, has included actors, journalists, politicians, even a spy chief, some but not all of them authors as well.

The actual process of narrowing down some 100-plus books to a manageable dozen has been described to me, by a recent juror, as a "pleasurable trickle of new reading experiences which escalates as the months go by into a panic-inducing flood – early meetings with just thirty novels to discuss are followed by huge bundles to consume by the early summer".

Another key participant, who has been involved in the process for several years, described wide variations in the approach of the jury chairpersons: "Some are impressively scientific, with elaborate, multilayered league tables; others are more intuitive, with gentle guidance of their teams, and gradual consensus building. There is no standard approach."

Clearly, doing justice to this flood requires great stamina, and with no permissible blunting of the senses. Most if not all the panel will be holding down busy other occupations. Yet the briefings I have had, from several sources, suggest that neither dissension from within nor criticism from without has been felt to be especially serious or justified.

There have been moments of potential division, of course. It would suggest a wholly artificial and superficial process if it were otherwise. A previously discarded entry might be rescued from obscurity by persuasive later advocacy, for example, but the other four would have to agree.

There are only rudimentary rules to follow, but the process since the inception of the prize in 1969 has been remarkably free of sustained criticism.

There was a revealing incident in July 2011 when that year's shortlist was announced at a packed press conference. Cross-examined on the significance of various criteria for their selection, the panel admitted, rather as an afterthought, that they attached some importance to books that are 'readable'. The London 'literati' (in the words of one observer) "went wild, interpreting this as dumbing down," with various snide references to the perceived prejudices of the jurors. However, by the time The Sense of an Ending, by Julian Barnes, was announced to be the winner on 18 October 2011 this elitist reaction had long since dissipated.

Summing up her team's decision, the chairperson of the judges said of the book, "It is exquisitely written, subtly plotted and reveals new depths with each reading." That's pretty straightforward.

The 2012 shortlist produced a different, and arguably rather artificial, complaint: the judges identified merit in books which seemed to demand a second reading. Critics jumped on this as implying that the plot of the novel, especially where there was a sting in the tail or an unexpected and subtle evolution, was of less importance than the sheer quality of the writing. Would that depress the chances of some of our most creative plotters?

Similarly, there were unfavourable comments on the prevalence of historical novels. Given the truly exhaustive research (admittedly brought to life by equally brilliant imagination) in Hilary Mantel's Wolf Hall and Bring up the Bodies, this was a curious reaction. Anyone who has read these (as I have recently) must surely accept their justified presence on the shortlist. The former gained the prize in 2010 by three votes to two, after the bookies had made it the favourite. The descent of the prize into betting-shop fodder again caused controversy in 2012.

We were told then that 147 entries were considered, and after shortlisting 'six extraordinary pieces of English prose' it took a further two hours and sixteen minutes for

Mantel's further extraordinarily powerful exploration of the career of Thomas Cromwell to surface as the winner. This verdict caused some ripples amongst the literati, but the public seemed satisfied.

No doubt the sponsors of the prize are only too happy that there is some critical controversy if it attracts attention.

However, there is a mystery hidden away in this decision-making process. At every stage and in every possible way all involved are reminded that 'The Man Booker Prize is for a Book not for an Author.'

The announcement of the 2012 award seemed again to ignore this reminder, as the media trumpeted, 'Hilary Mantel makes history as bloody tale of Tudor times wins her second Man Booker Prize – The 60-year-old becomes first woman to be recognised twice by judges.' Sir Peter Stothard, chairman of the judges panel, hailed her as "the greatest English prose writer eligible for the prize". The emphasis was all on the producer rather than the product.

And yet those who follow the proceedings all too often fall into that trap. Why? Perhaps here is a clue. The official press release in October 2011 began:

> Bookies' favourite, Julian Barnes, triumphs with Man Booker Prize win: Julian Barnes is tonight (Tuesday 18 October) named the winner of this year's £50,000 Man Booker Prize for Fiction. . . .

And the October 2012 headline announcement was scarcely less misleading: 'Hilary Mantel wins Man Booker Prize'.

With that leadership who can blame us for concluding that the purpose is not to encourage us to read good novels, but rather to bolster the pervasive celebrity culture of our times?

COALITION OR NO COALITION?

Edgar Anstey writes:

Also implicit in the concept of a committee is the doctrine of collective responsibility. By this is meant that after there has been full and free discussion of a matter, a group decision is reached which is regarded as a shared decision to be accepted loyally by all. Each member of the committee is then prepared (whatever personal reservations he may feel) to support the group decision and any action arising from it against possible attack from outside the group. If the committee does well, each member can take credit for its success. If it makes a mistake, the blame attached to any one member is reduced by being shared with the rest.

It may be of interest to digress for a few moments and note the rather different emphasis placed on collective responsibility in the USA and in Britain. In the UK this doctrine is stressed in all committees from the highest to the lowest. The emphasis on collective responsibility for Cabinet decisions derives from the responsibility of the Executive to Parliament, and is explained in the ancient saying 'If we don't hang together, we shall all be hanged separately'. In the USA, where under the constitution the Executive is not responsible to Congress, the tradition of collective responsibility is less strong. In matters of government the Americans are more inclined, by history and by temperament, to look for decisions by a leader, when the British would look for decisions by a group of people.

Committees, p.14

At about 8 p.m. on Friday 1 March 1974 I was elected MP for the Bodmin consitituency by a majority of just nine votes. The count had taken more than twelve hours, with six recounts, and we were locked into the Public Rooms at Liskeard with very little idea of what was happening in Westminster. Long before mobile phones we were dependent on the limited news brought in by friendly police officers alongside a supply of pasties. My mother (aged seventy-two) had engaged obstreperous young Conservatives with fisticuffs, our daughter (aged nineteen months) was entertaining the supporters at the Liberal Club and it was threatening to snow.

Outside, the news bulletins were speculating that, having challenged the nation with his "Who governs Britain?", Edward Heath had received the answer "Not you!" In the wake of the three-day week the Conservative government had lost 1.1 million votes since 1970, and thirty-three MPs. Labour had lost half a million votes, but gained ten extra MPs, and the Liberals had gained 3.9 million votes, but only an additional eight MPs. More significantly, neither Heath nor Harold Wilson looked like achieving the magic number of 318 for a majority in the Commons. Hence every result was of interest. Throughout the day, we were told when we eventually emerged to be chaired through the snowy crowd, those bulletins had ended with "and there is another recount in Bodmin".

By the following morning the media had done their sums. Labour with 301 MPs could not outvote 296 Conservatives, fourteen Liberals and twenty-four 'Others' (eleven Ulster Unionists, seven Scottish Nationalists, two Plaid Cymru, one SDLP, one Independent Labour, one Campaign for Social Democracy, and the outgoing Speaker). Even if all the natural allies in this disparate group could be won over, Labour had not won power. But nor could the Conservatives remain in office on their own. This was to be a hung parliament.

There is said to be a long-standing convention in British politics that the incumbent Prime Minister has the first chance of forming a government. Edward Heath and Jeremy Thorpe have both written since, with the benefit of hindsight, their accounts of what happened next. I prefer the meticulous contemporary memorandum of Robert Armstrong, then private secretary to the Prime Minister, but now a colleague in the Lords, and my own memory.[1]

At the time, as the Saturday speculation grew, we were engaged in the traditional victory tour that Cornish Liberals so enjoy, visiting some eighty different communities to thank supporters. At each stop the anxiety became more evident: "We didn't vote for you just to prop up Heath and the Tories" was the refrain. Since those who would have been Labour elsewhere, but plumped for the Liberals in Cornwall with what we would now call a tactical vote, were more than responsible for my wafer-thin majority, this was a powerful message. In any case, the radical Liberal tradition of the Duchy did not take kindly to the idea of providing a lifeboat to the sinking Tories.

They had good reason to be concerned. At midnight the previous evening the Prime Minister had spoken to Jeremy Thorpe, fresh from his own torchlit victory procession in Barnstaple, asking the Liberal leader to join him at No. 10 on that Saturday. Heath had insisted that the meeting should be private, which Thorpe later admitted was a mistake since many Liberals panicked, thinking that he was 'about to sacrifice the very independence of the party which I had spent twenty-five years working to preserve'.[2]

The lack of effective electronic communication added to the total absence of preparation for this outcome in causing misunderstanding.

David Steel was touring his Borders constituency to thank supporters when he heard on the car radio of Heath's invitation to Thorpe and "It is believed that David Steel, the Liberal Party Chief Whip, is also on his way to London."

1   Robert Armstrong, 'SECRET: Note for the Record – Events Leading to the Resignation of Mr Heath's Administration on 4 March 1974', 16 March 1974. The Margaret Thatcher Foundation says, 'The Armstrong memorandum was originally filed with papers on the fall of Heath in PREM 15/2069, but was missing when the documents were released in January 2005. It was finally located and opened following a FOI request by the Margaret Thatcher Foundation.'
2   J. Thorpe, *In My Own Time* (London: Politicos, 1999).

He said to his wife, "I'd better go there," and they handed over their two older children to the mother's help and set off with the baby in his carrycot.[3]

Over that weekend it became all too apparent that Heath was prevented by party paranoia from offering anything at all to address the patent absurdity of the electoral system. His hopes of stitching together a sustainable alliance of reliable votes in the Commons were doomed to failure. Typically, the Tory high command evidently thought that the lure of a Cabinet post (perhaps the Home Office or the Foreign Office) for the Liberal leader would be sufficient to overcome any residual organisation or policy misgivings in the rest of the party.

At the time, the media represented Thorpe as being the power-hungry enthusiast for a deal. The Armstrong memorandum makes it abundantly clear that the boot was on the other foot. Heath went to considerable lengths, encouraged by his inner Cabinet, to remain in office, even taking seriously an incredible offer of support from the eleven Ulster Unionist MPs, who were implacably opposed to his policies for Northern Ireland.

The meeting between Heath and Thorpe took place at 4 p.m. on Saturday 2 March, and was reported by Armstrong as follows:

> After about twenty minutes, when the Prime Minister had completed his opening analysis and invited Mr Thorpe to consider the possibility of some arrangement, Mr Thorpe had thanked him, made it clear that he could say nothing at that stage, had undertaken to consult his colleagues, and made as if to go. The Prime Minister had felt that the interview should not be cut so short, and had therefore gone over some of the ground in detail. Mr Thorpe had made another attempt to leave at about 4.45pm, and this too had been frustrated.[4]

The mood of the Tory high command, before a second, late

---

3   D. Steel, *Against Goliath* (London: George Weidenfield & Nicolson Ltd, 1989).

4   Robert Armstrong, 'SECRET: Note for the Record – Events Leading to the Resignation of Mr Heath's Administration on 4 March 1974'.

night, meeting between the two leaders that Sunday, is admirably summarised by Armstrong:

> There were significant disadvantages about a coalition with the Liberals, in that it would give the Liberals a veto over the whole of the Government's programme, and would involve some sort of commitment on electoral reform which very few Conservatives would be keen to offer and many might refuse to support, however cautious and qualified it might be. But these disadvantages were in the judgement of the colleagues present and (as the previous day's discussions had shown) of the Cabinet, outweighed by the disadvantages of allowing the Labour Party to form a Government.[5]

Heath and Thorpe met again between 10.30 p.m. and 11 p.m. Then the Monday morning Cabinet meeting 'took longer than expected' arguing over the terms of any commitment to examine the case for voting reform. In other words, the electoral self-interest of the Conservative Party took precedence over all else – as usual.

By the time the fourteen Liberal MPs met in a subterranean interview room in the House of Commons on the Monday morning the decision had almost been taken for us. Without a specific commitment to redress the electoral swindle perpetrated on voters, and without the arithmetic security to drive it through the Commons, there was no deal to be done. We concluded this discussion in about ten minutes.

There was then a dilemma. We could hardly emerge so quickly, and give the impression that we had treated the national crisis with such speedy nonchalance. In any case, long before 24/7 media coverage, the only likely journalist to be available at such a time on a Monday morning, with Parliament still dissolved, was Chris Moncrieff of the Press Association, and he wasn't due to take our statement for another three-quarters of an hour. We spent the time looking

---

5   Robert Armstrong, 'SECRET: Note for the Record – Events Leading to the Resignation of Mr Heath's Administration on 4 March 1974'.

back and looking forward: Jo Grimond reminded us, from his experience of the small government majority in the 1950–51 Parliament, that we were in for a summer of long nights, narrow votes and another election in the autumn. He and Steel emphasised that sooner or later we would have to think in terms of working with one or other of the two bigger parties in government. The likelihood of the Liberals somersaulting from third place to an overall majority in the Commons was fanciful in the extreme.

Eventually we issued our statement, rejecting Heath's overtures as unrealistic, and instead urging a three-party 'government of national unity' for a fixed period to tackle the economic crisis.

We had little optimism that this idea would go anywhere. Within hours Heath had resigned and Harold Wilson, who had craftily stayed mum throughout the media speculation, had been called to the palace and had formed a minority administration.

Fast forward to 2010.

In contrast to February 1974, the Liberal Democrat leadership prepared meticulously for a possible hung parliament. No doubt they benefitted from the history lessons of those of us who survived 1974, the later Lib–Lab Pact and the later-still Ashdown–Blair discussions. At the end of 2009 Nick Clegg invited four of his MP colleagues – Danny Alexander, Chris Huhne, David Laws and Andrew Stunell – to plan for such an outcome, and to be the core negotiating team if it actually happened.[6]

Necessarily, this process was shrouded in secrecy, but its existence was both presumed by and reassuring to those who

6   The most comprehensive first-hand account of the planning process – and subsequent negotiations with both the other parties – is given in David Laws' *22 Days in May* (London: Biteback, 2010), which also benefitted from Alison Suttie's meticulous contemporary note-taking. I cannot possibly do better than refer the reader to this account. My concern here is to highlight the contrast between the collective decision-making on one side and the almost Napoleonic leadership on the other.

read the runes or studied the small print of the opinion polls. You didn't need to be a professional psephologist to realise that, while Gordon Brown was almost certain to be heading for defeat, the vagaries of the electoral system meant David Cameron had an almost impossible swing to achieve if he was to form a majority administration. I, and no doubt many others in the party, contributed some ideas to the process, but all the really hard thinking was left to this quartet. Very sensibly, Clegg himself stayed at one remove from the detailed discussions, and indicated he would do the same if and when negotiations with another party took place.

The party, too, had felt the need for careful preparation. Following the abortive discussions in the run-up to the 1997 election, between Tony Blair and Paddy Ashdown, Liberal Democrats at all levels were understandably nervous about any deal that seemed to compromise the party's independence. At their 1998 conference in Southport an elaborate 'triple lock' motion was agreed, constraining the leadership's freedom of movement.

In brief, the consent of 75% of the MPs and of the federal executive was required to avoid the necessity of a special conference of official representatives of the whole membership. If a bare majority of the MPs and executive was all that was achieved, a special such conference had to give the proposals a two-thirds majority. If that conference could only produce a bare majority, then the approval of the whole membership in a postal ballot was required. The triple lock was designed to check any impetuous charge into alliances by Captain Ashdown, but his successor as leader in 2010 (and the potential negotiating team) was acutely aware of its significance.

We were not alone in preparing for stalemate. Whether by direction from his leader, or merely with his encouragement, Oliver Letwin clearly invested a great deal of time and intellectual analysis in investigating different scenarios. Indeed, he seemed better informed on Liberal Democrat policies, priorities and manifesto promises than our own MPs.

By contrast, all the contemporary and subsequent accounts suggest that the Labour leadership were in complete denial: some didn't want to admit to the possibility of defeat and others regarded the 'Liberals' (as Brown always contemptuously referred to us) as a sort of wholly owned subsidiary, who would have to prop them up if they failed to retain their overall majority.

My own involvement in the actual general election campaign was minuscule, at least compared with every other contest since 1964. We had just moved away from Cornwall, where my successor as MP no longer needed a ghost from the past to confuse the supporters, and we had built a very modern house with inevitable teething problems; a very different new team were at the helm at the national level.

So, apart from some local campaigning in Cheltenham, my only material contribution was to prepare similar but subtly different letters to appear in the four main national papers on the Saturday following polling (it made *The Telegraph* and *The Independent*). I argued that, in the event of no party securing a majority, there should be early legislation to prevent a Prime Minister seeking a dissolution for his own party advantage, when the nation clearly needed some stability and continuity to deal with the worsening economic situation. Naturally, I had in mind the Wilson ploy of the summer of 1974, when he postponed necessary but unpopular decisions in the hope of gaining a majority. My case for a Fixed-Term Parliament Bill was given immediate support in the subsequent Coalition Agreement and then by Parliament itself.

After some fifty years of campaigning, however, nothing would have kept me away when – that weekend – Nick Clegg reiterated his commitment to authorise negotiations with the party which had gained the most seats, the Conservatives. He told the quartet, "After my statement the ball is now firmly in David Cameron's court. As we agreed in our election planning, I expect David Cameron to appear painfully reasonable while preparing for a second general election."[7]

7   David Laws, *22 Days in May*, p.42.

That was not to be. One day we will find out just how and why Cameron was able to move so fast, and so decisively, to kill off within his party any idea of it forming a minority administration and daring us to bring it down. His 'big, open and comprehensive offer' to the Liberal Democrats that Friday afternoon was an eye-opener for his own MPs, for sceptical Liberal Democrats and for a bemused media.

There was such a flurry of formal consultation amongst the newly elected Liberal Democrat MPs, a majority of our peers and representatives of the party executive over the next seventy-two hours that it is now difficult to identify precisely when the decisive moment came. Our four negotiators reported back on that Saturday morning, first to the shadow Cabinet and then to the parliamentary party, in the rather spartan conference room of Local Government House in Smith Square. They gave a very full analysis of the initial response of both the other parties.

The latter meeting effectively endorsed the implicit rejection of one option by our shadow Cabinet earlier: nobody saw any merit in doing nothing, sitting on the Opposition benches in both Houses, waiting for an inevitable second election. That left us with three other options. We could sign up to a 'confidence and supply agreement' with the largest party, the Conservatives, but that too would lead to economic instability and probably an early election too; we could seek a full-scale coalition with them, which would incur a whole set of other risks; or we could try to cobble together a rainbow coalition with Labour and enough minority party MPs to ensure a hope of continuous majorities in the Commons.

This last option had already been denounced by the media as a 'coalition of the losers'.

Sunday was spent – by those not actually engaged in the cross-party discussions – in informal conversations to gauge the likely response of key figures inside and outside Parliament.

My sole contribution throughout – informally and in the formal meetings too – was to draw on my experience, both of short-term minority governments and as a previous Chief Whip, to underline the importance of the arithmetic: without the constant support of sufficient numbers of MPs, over a realistic period of at least four years, a government would be doomed to failure. "My heart may be with Labour but – despite years of campaigning against them – my head tells me we have to work with the Tories" – scarcely an original comment.

Indeed, Paddy Ashdown, appearing on that Sunday's *Andrew Marr Show*, put it more neatly: "The British electorate have invented an exquisite method of torture for the Lib Dems: our instincts go one way; the mathematics go the other."

Meanwhile, however, Gordon Brown in No. 10 – as we know now from Andrew Adonis's *Five Days in May*[8], published three years afterwards – had persuaded himself, and some of his colleagues, that the parliamentary arithmetic either could be surmounted or did not matter. I shall return to the Adonis interpretation of these events later.

By the time of the next full consultative meeting, at 10.30 p.m. on Monday 10 May, there had been substantial developments. Peers and MPs had met separately during the day, just to be kept abreast of the twists and turns of the various discussions going on further up Whitehall.

The MPs, peers and federal-executive representatives met in the Grand Committee Room, off Westminster Hall, which was more suited to the gravity of the decisions awaiting us, as its name implies. The quartet – and Nick himself – reported on the widening differences of response from Brown and his team on the one hand and Cameron, Hague, Letwin and Osborne on the other.

The former had alternated from desperate lecturing (Brown) to differing enthusiasm for compromise (Mandelson and Adonis were especially keen while Balls, Miliband and Harman seemed more cautious, perhaps only too willing to go into Opposition). The Conservatives were businesslike and

---

8 A. Adonis, *Five Days in May: The Coalition and Beyond* (London: Biteback, May 2013).

very keen to avoid more years out of office.

By this time, Gordon Brown had hinted at his intended resignation and yet Cameron had convinced himself – and his key colleagues – that only a specific commitment to a referendum on some form of electoral reform could create conditions for a stable, sustainable coalition with the Liberal Democrats. The details had yet to be concluded, but the atmosphere of our meeting was noticeably more upbeat. Sceptics – especially amongst those peers whose previous careers had included much stronger links to the Labour Party than to our traditional enemies in the Tory ranks – were beginning to show more enthusiasm. Vince Cable too said he thought an agreement with the Conservatives was the only viable option.

After one more attempt at a serious conversation with the Labour representatives on the Tuesday morning, which proved even more frustrating now they were effectively leaderless and reconciled to 'oppositionitis', the negotiations with the Conservatives were under huge pressure to deliver. By 8 p.m. Brown had been to the palace to resign, and by 8.30 Cameron had agreed to try to form a government, but still nobody could be sure that it would be a coalition. Remember the triple lock!

After 9.30 a final meeting of Liberal Democrat MPs, peers and executive members got under way at Local Government House. The consensus was well summed up by Ashdown, who said that he found it difficult to abandon his dream of a realignment of the left, with such obvious risks to the party, and his inclination had been to bow out of politics altogether, and concentrate on his garden and grandchildren.

However, after telling Nick my decision earlier today, I took the time to actually read the document which you have negotiated. I have to say that it is magnificent. Amazing. F*** it. How can I stay out of this fight? You know that I cannot resist a battle, not least in the company of friends?[9]

A matter of minutes later there were three separate votes, each

9 D. Laws, *22 Days in May*, p.197.

with a dramatic show of hands. The MPs voted 50 to nil in favour, the peers 31 to nil, the executive members 27 to 1.

Could it have gone the other way? Could the discussions with the Labour team have delivered? Adonis, in retrospect, clearly thinks they could. However, even he – optimist for plural politics as he has always been – put his finger on three major obstacles.[10]

First, Gordon Brown's obsessive claims, that Friday and Saturday, that he could stitch together a stable majority in the Commons are dubious (he never was that good with figures) and Adonis skips lightly over the obvious difficulties. My memories of the 1974 impasse, which neither of them had experienced, suggested an inevitable lurch from crisis to crisis each week, further pressure on the pound and another election in the autumn.

Secondly, we had correctly appreciated the relative enthusiasm of our suitors. Again, Adonis admits the obvious. After David Blunket, John Reid and Andy Burnham had gone public on their opposition to a deal, echoing private reservations in the Cabinet by political heavyweights like Jack Straw, he records sadly of the Tories, 'Their side was desperate for power; too many on ours were desperate for opposition.' Knowing the parlous state of the country's finances, Liam Byrne (author of the notorious note to his successor as Chief Secretary at the Treasury stating, 'There is no money . . . good luck') was one of those to prefer the exit door.

Thirdly, the role and character of Brown was itself a major obstacle, as Adonis (and Mandelson) realised from the outset. It was not just that he was the Prime Minister who had just lost an election – much like Edward Heath in 1974 – but that his whole personality seemed so much at variance with the consensual, collegiate and cooperative skill set he would need to deal with the challenges ahead. His habitual condescension to Clegg and all Liberal Democrats, never bringing himself to call us anything other than 'the Liberals', grated even with his own colleagues. Throughout the post-election discussions

10 A. Adonis, *Five Days in May: The Coalition and Beyond*, p.111.

and meetings he seemed to assume that, eventually, common antipathy for the Tory enemy would swing the wholly owned subsidiary into his embrace.

Even when Brown announced his intention to resign, in due course, the momentum, and the other factors identified by Adonis, had swung the outcome in the other direction. However, that was not to be the end of our consultative process. Clegg and the party officers had already decided they wanted the membership conference to debate and endorse the Coalition Agreement. While this was technically unnecessary it was surely a very adroit move to make sure there was the widest possible commitment to the agreement.

So on Sunday 16 May we all trooped off to the National Exhibition Centre, outside Birmingham, for a special conference, organised at four days' notice, with a record 1,650 representatives. After more than three hours of debate and sixty-eight contributions (only six against the motion) the conference endorsed the coalition by an overwhelming majority, with only a dozen or so dissenters.

If you have lost track of the tortuous consultation process, I don't blame you; it was truly exhaustive and (for some) exhausting, immediately after a draining election campaign.

From then on the Liberal Democrats 'owned' that decision, and it had important repercussions later on. When the big rebellions took place – for example, over Lords reform – it was the Conservative MPs and activists who proved most ill-disciplined.

Indeed, they could claim (and several did claim) that they had never been given the opportunity to examine the issues or the eventual agreement in anything like the regular, detailed and truly consultative way that we Liberal Democrats had. There were also later complaints from the Conservative back benches when UCL calculated that 75% of the junior partner's manifesto had found its way into the Coalition Agreement against only 60% of their own.

The timing of the different stages of coalition negotiations were undoubtedly significant. Those meetings with the Conservative shadow Cabinet and the bulk of their parliamentary party on the afternoon and early evening of Monday 10 May were clearly intended by Cameron to clear out of the way the feasibility of a limited confidence-and-supply agreement with the Liberal Democrats for a minority administration. At that juncture it seemed that the on–off discussions with Labour might be getting somewhere, with Brown indicating that he was prepared to step aside. So the pressure was on: Cameron and his MPs might well think that the chance of re-entry into No. 10 might be slipping away.

For obvious reasons I have no personal eye-witness account of the meetings that David Cameron held with his MPs. The most authoritative descriptions would seem to be those in *5 Days to Power* by Rob Wilson[11], Conservative MP for Reading East and a former party whip and shadow minister.

He wrote of the leadership's tactical approach to an offer of an electoral-reform referendum: 'The matter was never put to a ballot, and it was never suggested to Chief Whip Patrick McLoughin by any member of the Parliamentary Party that it should be . . .' However, he reported that 'There was an undercurrent in the meeting that a minority Conservative government would be a preferable outcome to a coalition with the Liberal Democrats.'[12]

The next and conclusive meeting with the MPs (no peers as far as I can discover) took place *after* Cameron had been to the palace, accepted from the Queen the commission to form a government and announced his intention of making it a full coalition.

Again, Wilson sums up the mood: 'Cameron made a typically impressive speech, but in contrast to the Liberal Democrats there was no detailed discussion, let alone a vote on, the Coalition Agreement or any of its individual provisions. Cameron was none the less treated to another standing ovation as he left the room.'[13]

11 R. Wilson, *5 Days to Power* (London: Biteback, 2010).
12 Ibid.
13 Ibid.

It was indeed, by then, a fait accompli as far as the leadership were concerned. Their MPs did not 'own' the agreement, either in principle or in detail.

That contrast speaks volumes for the essential difference between the Conservative and Liberal Democrat Parties. And it would also prove very significant for the future relationship between them.

In the context of May 2010 decision-making, the Conservatives would seem to have followed the American tradition Anstey described, while the Liberal Democrats were typically British, almost to a fault.

The Committee is Essential to The Democratic Way of Life.

CASE STUDY: REFORM OF THE HOUSE OF LORDS

Edgar Anstey writes:

A final piece of advice, based on observations of people with high intelligence and strong personalities who have learned to make the most effective use of committees on which they have served: if you are the dominant member of a committee (especially if you are not the Chairman) it is essential that you should avoid making this fact too obvious. If you are wise, therefore, you will go out of your way to invite the co-operation of other members and to let them have as much credit as possible for what they do.

In particular:

(a) Develop your successive ideas, as far as possible in association with each other member of the committee in turn, and let each idea be credited to the pair of you, not just to you alone. Your ideas may well be improved by your colleague's comments but, even if they are not, to seek co-operation in this way makes for increased friendliness.

(b) When you have developed an idea in partnership with a colleague, invite him to present the actual proposal, then support it yourself.

(c) When quoting a good point made at a past meeting, attribute it to the appropriate committee member by name, even if the point was partly your own.

Ready appreciation of past contributions by your colleagues is likely to encourage their maximum co-operation in future.

Committees, pp.79–80

The preamble to the 1911 Parliament Act stated baldly, 'Whereas it is intended to substitute for the House of Lords as it at present exists a second chamber constituted on a popular instead of a hereditary basis but such a substitution cannot immediately be brought into operation,' before launching into its detailed provisions.

Over 100 years later we may – or may not – be about to realise that intention. The rocky road of reform was perhaps best illustrated by Clement Attlee's characteristic summary, reported as follows in the papers of one of the most radical Cabinets of the century:

> In matters of constitutional reform there were great dangers in trying to be too logical. It was more in accordance with British traditions to build on the past by adapting existing institutions, however illogical that course might be.[1]

Previous suggestions that the Lords should be abolished quietly disappeared.

Since then repeated manifesto commitments have come and gone. In 1958 the hereditary (and male) monopoly was demolished with the Life Peerages Act, but no attempt to fulfil the 1911 commitment was even contemplated. In 1968 the Wilson government was thwarted by an unholy alliance of two formidable orators: Michael Foot (who would have preferred abolition to giving the Lords democratic legitimacy) and Enoch Powell (who resolutely opposed any further change).

In his pre-victory book *New Britain: My Vision of a Young Country*[2] Tony Blair wrote, 'The party I lead will carry out

1 Cabinet papers released by National Archives – CAB 128/12/1, held on 6 January 1948.
2 T. Blair, *New Britain: My Vision of a Young Country* (London: Fourth Estate, 1996).

in government the programme we provide in our manifesto beforehand. Nothing more, nothing less, that is my word,' and he promised 'an end to hereditary peers sitting in the House of Lords, as a first step to a proper directly elected second chamber, and the chance for the people to decide after the election the system by which they elect the Government of the future'. At Prime Minister's Questions on 9 February 2005, I asked him which of these promises he most regretted breaking. Naturally, I didn't get a straight answer then, and didn't expect one, any more than we got legislation to make good on those commitments.

Instead, there were seemingly interminable committees and commissions. The Royal Commission, chaired by Lord Wakeham, reporting in January 2000, was too tentative for the radicals and too radical for Blair and the Cabinet. A joint committee (described above) fared no better. Our cross-party group's attempt to revive the reform momentum, in the run-up to the 2005 general election, only secured some limited manifesto commitments.

However, in February 2007, the government published a further White Paper, appearing to concede the case for a fifty-fifty split between appointed and elected members, despite Blair's antagonism to a hybrid House.[3] On 7 March 2007 MPs voted by comfortable margins both for the 80%-elected option (by 305 to 267) and for the fully elected option (by 337 to 224). The reform agenda was back on the rails.

Naturally, peers voted in the opposite direction, and later asserted that the Commons majorities were tainted by opportunism! Some MPs had voted for both a fully appointed and a fully elected House, because they opposed all the hybrid options. Yet, in an attempt to undermine the significance of the majorities, peers later claimed this indicated dissent from the whole reform agenda, which hung on acceptance of a mixed solution. The MPs' votes, they argued, should not be taken at face value, but carefully interpreted as an attempt to derail progress.

3   HC Deb, 29 January 2003, col.877 (Q6).

Jack Straw's subsequent White Paper, published in July 2008, saw the light of day only because the majority of his colleagues in Gordon Brown's Cabinet were quite convinced that its reform proposals would go no further.

Like so much of the Brown constitutional-reform agenda – conceived simply to differentiate his regime from Blair's indifference – all this was soon submerged by the banking crisis, the credit crunch and the Prime Minister's retreat into his paranoid bunker.

In the May 2010 general election, however, an entirely new scenario emerged: all three major parties gave manifesto promises to implement reform of the Lords. The Conservatives committed themselves to 'work to build a consensus for a mainly-elected second chamber to replace the current House of Lords'. Labour were more specific with 'We will ensure that the hereditary principle is removed from the House of Lords. Further democratic reform to create a fully elected Second Chamber will then be achieved in stages,' although the party also introduced the idea of a confirmatory referendum.

The Liberal Democrats reiterated the intention to 'replace the House of Lords with a fully elected second chamber with considerably fewer members than the current House'.

In the following coalition negotiations between the Conservative and Liberal Democrat teams there was no great difficulty in reconciling the different emphases, and the agreement merely noted:

We agree to establish a committee to bring forward proposals for a wholly or mainly elected upper chamber on the basis of proportional representation. The committee will come forward with a draft motion by December 2010. It is likely that this bill will advocate single long terms of office. It is also likely there will be a grandfathering system for the current Lords. In the interim, Lords appointments will be made with the objective of creating a second chamber reflective of the share of the vote secured by the political parties in the last general election.

David Laws recollects no controversy between the party representatives on this item.[4]

With the Labour Party ostensibly on board, as soon as their leadership and shadow Cabinet dispositions were in place, Deputy Prime Minister Nick Clegg steered a cross-party group towards a White Paper and draft bill in May 2011. As agreed at the birth of the coalition a joint committee of MPs and peers was to consider these proposals.

What follows is a near-contemporary series of notes of the way in which the committee was brought into being and its subsequent work. Admittedly, these were from my own viewpoint, at the time, but (I suggest) they are as honest an assessment of the way it has grappled with this previously intractable problem as any. And I hope they give a realistic appraisal of the strengths and weaknesses of scrutiny by parliamentary committees.

4 April 2011: Before the government's proposals even appeared there were ominous portents. First, a *Times* article, apparently leaked by the Conservative participants, forecast its main features. Most of these were reiterating agreed elements of the Straw White Paper, and indeed the *Breaking the Deadlock* cross-party bill, but the reference to a much smaller House – reduced to just 300 – caused me real concern.

27 April: I arranged a meeting with Nick Clegg, accompanied by my colleague Lord (Chris) Rennard, for later in the month. We explained that such a small House, with probably only eighty elected in each tranche, would produce an unrepresentative membership, deprived of gender and ethnic diversity. The fewer people there are in a group (especially one elected by the public), the more unlikely it is that diversity will be achieved. I noted, too, that the cross-benchers would respond very badly to only twenty appointees each time, while there would be a public as well as parliamentary outcry at the idea that all these members

4   D. Laws, *22 Days in May*, p.97.

would have to be full-time to get the necessary work done. Few people, in Westminster let alone in the country at large, seemed to want the second chamber to be packed with full-time politicians like the Commons.

Nick said he was surprised that nobody had expressed these reservations to him previously. Chris and I bit our tongues, and didn't observe that nobody had asked us.

10 May: Subsequently, the Leader of the Lords, Lord (Tom) Strathclyde, invited me in to discuss the then imminent White Paper. He too expressed concern at the references to just 300 'full-time' parliamentarians. We agreed it was an unnecessary hostage to fortune, but by then the White Paper and draft bill were on their way to the printers. This was not an encouraging prelude to the publication.

17 May: White Paper and draft bill published: in their joint introduction David Cameron and Nick Clegg were specific: "We are both strongly persuaded that this is a unique opportunity for our country to instil greater democracy into our institutions and are fully committed to holding the first elections to the reformed House of Lords in 2015." Not much room for manoeuvre there. However, the real surprise was the enthusiastic endorsement of the whole Cabinet. Theresa May, Liam Fox and George Osborne all took to the airwaves in support of reform.[5]

17 & 21 June: Proposed membership of the joint committee comprises thirteen MPs and thirteen peers, ten of whom will be Conservatives, nine Labour, three Liberal Democrats, two cross-bench peers, one bishop and one Democratic Unionist. The ratio reflects the arithmetic in each House, as always, but that is not the issue in this case. The party line is scarcely relevant when there are so many who refuse to support their leaders' manifesto commitments.

5   J. Pickard and A. Barker, 'Tories Speak Up for Lords Elections', *Financial Times*, 17 May 2011.

21–22 & 27 June: The Lords and Commons stage 'take note' debates on the White Paper and draft bill, the former on 21 and 22 June 2011 and the latter on 27 June 2011. On both occasions, and especially from Their Lordships, there was a steady stream of nitpicking and St Augustinian procrastination ("Lord, make us virtuous, but not yet"). However, eventually the promised joint committee of peers and MPs are appointed, by resolution in both Houses, to undertake the scrutiny role of the draft bill, taking account of the options referred to in the White Paper. For the first time for several decades Parliament is faced with specific legislative proposals. And since I am nominated to this committee, I will be trying to build a consensual team, with colleagues from all parties and both Houses, to achieve a workable outcome.

And this is where Edgar Anstey's advice comes in.

5 July: Informal discussion with Lord (Ivor) Richard[6], who seems destined to chair the committee. Only moderately encouraging, since he clearly envisages a protracted process, to keep the most reluctant members on board. Since I had previously urged Clegg, and through him the PM, to see if Lord (Andrew) Adonis[7] would take on the chairmanship – and got some way in persuading him to accept – this is discouraging. Ivor has an impeccable record of support for democratic reform, but is he prepared to lead, or does he want simply to go with the slow flow?

6–7 July: My astute parliamentary assistant, Alex, and I have trawled through the Hansard reports, and any other relevant material we can lay our hands on. We reckon that some ten of the now announced members of the joint committee are hardboiled opponents of reform, some ten are potential or declared supporters and the remaining six have yet to give any indication or may be persuadable. A recipe for gridlock or all to play for?

6   Lord Richard, Leader of the House of Lords for the first year of the Blair government, a former European Commissioner and former Labour MP.
7   Lord Adonis, a former Labour minister in the Brown and Blair governments.

11 July: First meeting of the committee. I can honestly say, as I report back to Alex and other colleagues, one of the most depressing of my entire political career (and that is saying something, since I spent three years chairing the executive of the old Liberal Party!).

I had suggested that we three Lib Dems (Baroness (Ros) Scott[8], John Thurso[9] and I) should carefully spread ourselves round the room, and not appear to be acting as any kind of clique. I sat beside Ann Coffey[10], an old reforming ally from committees in the Commons. We agreed to keep each other awake and cheerful in the coming months of tedium and time-wasting, if the reactionaries have their way.

The first evidence of this likely scenario was when the chairman suggested that we could not meet again until the second week in October. The long summer recess was thought to mean that our clerks wouldn't be able to prepare anything for us to examine. A new MP wondered aloud whether we should not have at least an outline work programme, aimed at completion for the planned reporting date. That was pooh-poohed as unrealistic. Then there was a suggestion that we should invite academics to paint in the historical background of the reform proposals. Finally, the very idea that we should invite the minister responsible – the highly intelligent Conservative MP Mark Harper – to set out the government's thinking on the draft bill at an early meeting was about to be kicked into touch, not least by Conservative peers.

I managed to square some of these confusing circles by persuading colleagues that we could at least get the academic contributions out of the way at a September meeting, and invite the minister to come as early as possible in October. The clerks, who had hitherto observed the delaying tactics with remarkable detachment, looked relieved.

---

8 Baroness Scott of Needham Market, Liberal Democrat Party president, 2009 and 2010.

9 John Thurso, formerly a member of the Lords by virtue of a hereditary peerage. Now Liberal Democrat MP for Caithness, Sutherland and Easter Ross.

10 Labour MP for Stockport.

However, after a remarkably short meeting, I stayed behind and made it my business to get to know the newer MPs I had not met before. They were all as dejected as I was. And Laura Sandys[11], one of the brightest Conservative new entrants of 2010, with whom I had worked many years previously on quite different legislation, was especially determined to push for more progress.

12–19 July: End of term, and too much else to do, but I have made time to meet both Ann Coffey and Laura Sandys, and (bless them) they have given up precious time to meet me. Both will be essential links with their Commons colleagues on the committee.

Laura has already prepared some ideas, which we mull over on the Lords Terrace, and agree to discuss again before Parliament resumes at the beginning of September.

Meanwhile, I sound out the clerks on the feasibility of at least an outline work programme. They are tentatively encouraging, but – as always – it is for the committee (and particularly its chairman) to decide.

A sideshow is developing. The much quoted Steel Bill, which many of the most resistant peers have grabbed hold of as a way of postponing full reform, is back in the fray. Lord (David) Steel[12] has always argued that his purpose is solely to achieve modest, agreed and urgent improvements (ending the hereditary by-elections, introducing more effective mechanisms to deal with errant members and for those who wish to retire, etc.) while waiting for the inevitably long process of comprehensive reform to be completed.

At the committee meeting the very idea that we might suggest to the government that they could usefully take on his bill was sat on smartly. But I happen to know that ministers are not now so resistant to this idea, since it would call the bluff of those (like ex-Speaker Baroness (Betty) Boothroyd) who want to keep using it as an excuse to refuse proper

11 Laura Sandys, Conservative MP for South Thanet.
12 Lord Steel of Aikwood, Leader of the Liberal Party from 1976 to 1988.

scrutiny of the government bill. David is lobbying hard for the government to sponsor his limited proposals, but some of his fair-weather friends seem now to be backing off. I wonder why?

5–6 September: Parliament resumes after the summer recess. Laura Sandys has revised her notes, with some suggestions from me. Unfortunately, still a determined smoker, she needs an open-air consultation, and the terrace is getting autumnal. We agree that she should circulate her ideas to all the committee members after next Monday's meeting, so that she should not look as if she is being too presumptuous. Ann Coffey is less complicated: a brief encounter at the coffee bar in Portcullis House provided enough time for an exchange of intelligence about our respective party colleagues.

A chance meeting with Ivor Richard in the cloakroom was more substantial. He told me, very confidentially, that Mark Harper has offered to meet the committee at its first evidence-taking session in October. I expressed delight and surprise in equal measure, the latter rather insincerely since I had specifically arranged with Mark that he should make this offer, fearing otherwise that the ministerial contribution would be deliberately delayed.

12 September: A quartet of academics gently lecture the committee on the history of the House of Lords, its origins and evolution and the attempts to reform it in the last 100 years. I sit next to Professor Lord (Peter) Hennessy[13], so that I can benefit from his very legible note-taking. However, he is so erudite that I can hardly keep up.

No great surprises from the session. I am (of course) prejudiced, but my friend Nicolas Baldwin – who has the advantage of past experience working in the Lords as well as solid political and historical research since – seems the most realistic. He knocks on the head the curious notion

13 Lord Hennessy of Nympsfield, Attlee Professor of Contemporary British History and author of a panoply of books on modern political history.

that no change in composition can be contemplated until the conventions governing the relationship between the two Houses are reviewed and revised. These have always evolved in response to other changes. Very impressive contribution from Chris Ballinger of Exeter College, my own alma mater, to whom I introduced myself afterwards. Another useful source of advice?

At the very end, just as our guests were packing their bags and committee members were shuffling their papers, the clerks distributed a green sheet. It lists a very helpful draft working programme aimed at the end of February 2012 as a target for report. Excellent – just what I lobbied for. But my eye was caught by the far right-hand column. Against Mark Harper's appearance is noted, 'Private (unless the Committee decide otherwise)'. Ever so modestly, with half the room probably not knowing what I was talking about, I suggested we should agree that this should be in public, since I am sure the minister would wish it so. Ivor absent-mindedly agreed, and it is so. Another casual victory but an important one. Until the responsible **Conservative** minister sets out publicly the full government case most of the Tory peers (and all of the Tory press) will perpetuate the myth that it is all a Clegg plot.

13 September: At dinner in the Home Room I found myself sitting alongside Viscount Astor. The Lords end of the building is more civilised than the Commons Members' Dining Room, where tables are jealously guarded and occupied on strictly tribal party lines. Here we sit with a complete cross-section of parties, factions and generations. He is distinguished by being the grandson of the formidable Nancy Astor, the first woman to sit in the Commons. He succeeded to his title at the age of twenty-one, since his father died when he was fourteen.

I suggested a quick chat afterwards because he is also closely related to a certain Mrs Cameron, and the PM (no less) has previously suggested to both of us that we keep in touch on Lords reform issues. We adjourned to the almost empty Peers'

Guest Room. Astor remains a tentative reformer – "I have absolutely no objection to bringing in some elected members" – but is rightly apprehensive about likely opposition and managing a transition process. "Our people here are almost all dyed-in-the-wool, and I keep telling Dave that it will be a hard slog." I have to agree.

14 September: After a very late contribution to a totally different debate I came out of the chamber just as Mark Harper was passing by. I gave him a precis of the Monday meeting, and we agree to talk again before his appearance before the committee in October.

6 October: By elaborate prior arrangement Mark, fresh from the Conservative Conference, phoned to discuss tactics for his appearance before the joint committee next Monday. We used a full forty minutes to review the likely line of questioning. I was able to sketch the current position of the Labour hierarchy – delay is the best way to cover their deep divisions – and encourage a little extra research by his team into the consistency of their White Paper and draft bill with the previous cross-party work led by Jack Straw. We agree that the continual carping about the primacy of the Commons, and the alleged need to codify the conventions relevant to the relationship between the two Houses, have long since been dealt with effectively. However, for a Conservative minister to disarm these objections may be very timely. Meanwhile, one of his party colleagues has been seduced into constant repetition of another red herring: indirect elections on the Dutch or Danish model. I suggested that Mark might like to describe this as only appropriate if the UK adopts a federal constitution, as favoured by Liberal Democrats. That should kill it quick. And he promises to get an update from his ministerial colleagues on the best way to deflect the Steel Bill proposals. He is such a reliably well-informed and polished performer, I look forward to Monday.

10 October: No great surprises – the Conservative members of the committee, especially the peers, are clearly disorientated by the sight and sound of a Conservative minister positively articulating the case for reform. The vast picture on the wall of Moses delivering the Ten Commandments to his bemused followers seems all too apt.

However, the only mood-changing moment occured after he had left us. Since we still had questions for Mr Harper, some members used this as an excuse to raise again the suggestion that we should demand an extension of time, beyond the agreed date at the end of February 2012. In the chair Ivor Richard himself seemed defeatist. Seated between a Labour and a Conservative MP, I gently encouraged both to protest. Surely we should meet for longer, or more often, rather than throw in the towel before we have really got going on our work programme? There were murmurs of agreement. I reminded colleagues of Parkinson's Law – work fills the time available – so if we allow ourselves until May, or July, or October, or 2015, we can certainly find ways to string out our scrutiny, but I want to achieve an outcome. It was agreed that the clerks will canvass options – longer sessions on Monday evenings or a second meeting each week on Thursdays perhaps. I can guarantee the latter will be unpopular. Meanwhile we have seen off the deliberately dilatory tendency, a real victory which I will report to Mark before he next appears before the committee.

1–10 November: All my behind-the-scenes negotiations with like-minded committee members looked doomed to failure when we had our first informal discussion of 'Theme A' (the relationship between the two Houses, powers, conventions and the primacy of the Commons) after yet another bravura performance by Mark on 7 November. Chairman Richard produced a curiously wide-ranging note, extending far beyond this theme. With support from allies, I tried to tie down a

---

14 Clause 2 of the draft bill stated baldly, 'Nothing in this Act . . . affects the primacy of the House of Commons.'

rejection of the much derided Clause 2[14] – nothing will change – in favour of a factual statement of the existing position as enshrined in the Parliament Acts, and a suggestion of a review when the reformed House reaches a tipping point – say, when 50% are elected. Despite some murmurs of support, the lateness of the hour spelt indecision.

However, on the following Thursday, at 3.40 an e-mail with attachments arrived from the clerks. Behold, a 'confidential annex' faithfully records this suggestion, with apparent approval. Moreover, my persistent concern about the practicality, electoral proportionality and popularity of a very small House of full-time parliamentarians was swept up in an agreement that 300 is 'too small' and 'around 450 would be appropriate'.

Almost before I had time to absorb these victories another e-mail arrived – sent at 3.55 – to 'recall' all these papers. In common, no doubt, with every other committee member I hastily checked to see what had changed when the revised batch arrived.

The 'confidential annex' has disappeared: cock-up or conspiracy? So the fuller discussion note I have been working on, setting out the background for a subsequent review of the conventions, went off to the clerks with the endorsement of seven other committee members.

14, 21 & 28 November: Seemingly interminable evidence sessions, with all the usual suspects repeating each others' prejudices to the committee. And yet Ivor Richard – whose chairmanship appears to be so laid-back as to be almost horizontal – is encouraging us to hear even more, mostly from peers who don't want to be reformed.

However, perhaps demonstrating well-disguised cunning, he nudged the majority, at this latter meeting, into accepting that he can request only one postponement for our report (from 29 February to 29 March 2012, the beginning of the Easter recess). This should put a stop to the endless procrastination some favour.

The discussion on electoral systems also advances minutely: lacking enthusiasm for either pure STV [the Single Transferable Vote system] or regional-list PR. There is some sympathy for Gavin Barwell[15], a new Conservative MP, who advocates a compromise which seeks to combine the best features of both – some simplicity for those who do not wish to choose between candidates, without denying electors that choice. In the break before the evidence session I undertook to draft some alternative ballot papers for him and other allies.

Then to an interrogation of the Archbishop of Canterbury[16]. I suggested that the survival of bishops in the Lords, a relic of their medieval role as huge feudal landowners and moneybags rather than anything to do with Henry VIII, the Reformation or the Established Church, is an anomaly and an anachronism. He accepted that it is and will be an anomaly in the reformed House but countered, with a twinkle, "I am afraid that anachronism is, to me, a shortcut in an argument." I am prostrate.

7 December: Briefing meeting with Nick Clegg at the Cabinet Office: unsurprisingly he arrived fresh from a Euro-tangle with the PM, and took a few minutes to cheer up. I was able to bring him up to date on the work of the committee, and our determination to report before the Easter recess, and his face lightened up. Talking tactics on the limited changes proposed in David Steel's bill was more problematic.

Nick is preparing a speech on his commitment to a more 'open society', with references to the reactionary forces which stand in the way of political reform, not least in the Lords. I got to make some modest suggestions on his tone and targets.

12 & 19 December: Just when the evidence sessions become monotonously repeated assertions we stumble on some genuine

15 Conservative MP for Croydon Central.
16 Rowan Williams, now Lord Williams of Oystermouth, PC.

expertise from academics Alan Renwick and Iain McLean on the last Monday before the recess. Their dispassionate analysis of the relative merits of STV and open lists is especially timely given the previous discussion, but we are in danger of drifting off into an intemperate debate on other issues. During the comfort break before our private 'deliberation' session I asked the chairman if we could not move straight on to the electoral-system discussion, and could I distribute a note? He agreed.

So I circulated the specimen ballot paper, dreamt up by Alex and me, which permits the less fastidious elector to vote for a party list 'above the line' while the more selective can choose between candidates, even across parties and independents, 'below the line'. Since it is Christmas we have merrily included all the committee members' names as candidates. I tactfully observed that this had been produced to meet the particular concerns of Oliver Heald[17], the lead Conservative MP present, who then expressed surprised support, and others followed suit. Jeff Rooker[18] wanted to reverse the order, and build in some complicated arithmetical advantage for the electoral anoraks.

I was just about to suggest that we ask the two academics to vet these ideas when the chairman said, "Well, that's agreed then." I was suitably flabbergasted.

We did not attempt the vexed question of Commons primacy, conventions and the Parliament Acts, because seven o'clock approached, and a special morning session in the New Year was agreed. On the way out several allies asked if I could arrange a pre-meeting. As the recess loomed, Alex managed to contact at least eight of our reforming colleagues for this purpose, and we updated the note previously endorsed so that it responds more directly to the chairman's questions on this topic.

17 Conservative MP for North-East Hertfordshire and a former shadow Leader of the Commons.
18 Lord Rooker, a former Labour minister in the Blair governments and former Labour MP.

21 December: Nick Clegg had a good day at Deputy Prime Minister's Questions yesterday, but peers are obsessed with his speech the day before. An oral question on the planned powers of the reformed House gave me a chance to put the record straight on our previous joint-committee[19] recommendations, but several opponents of reform – from Labour, Conservative and cross-benches – attempted feeble festive jokes at Nick's expense.

10 January 2012: First day back after the recess and eight of the reformers from the joint committee met to discuss tactics. We agreed to resist attempts to reopen the whole fractious issue of the relationship between Commons and Lords, and the 'primacy' of the former, by suggesting a simplified form of words describing the statutory position. The favoured ploy of the procrastinators is to insist on rewriting the law – or codifying the conventions – **before** any change in composition can be considered.

12 January: Our approach seems to be gaining ground, with the chairman clearly losing patience with the time-wasting of opponents at today's special 'deliberative' meeting. My co-reformers (now up to ten) agreed to submit a note setting out our approach to the primacy issue.

16 January: Newly enobled Lord (Patrick) Cormack[20] led his fan club in presenting evidence against the government's proposals to the committee. Challenged to explain what reforms they **would** support he cited a retirement scheme to reduce the overlarge size of the House, based on an age limit. I put on record the fact that only four of the existing peers are aged less than forty while nineteen are over ninety. He waffled about this for several minutes, but his more elderly

19 The Joint Committee on Conventions was convened in 2006 to examine and describe the conventions governing the relationship between the Lords and the Commons.
20 Lord Cormack, a former grandee of the House of Commons, a long-standing Conservative MP for Cannock and then South Staffordshire.

supporters, sitting behind him, began to look increasingly uncomfortable.

19 January: At another special meeting the majority eventually concluded that we should report briefly on the existing statutory relationship between the Houses, to give a factual analysis of Commons primacy, but not venture into speculation on its future evolution. This is a very solid advance, if we can maintain this majority for the main thrust of the bill as a result.

23–27 January: Another busy week on the reform issue, but less in the joint committee than in the corridors, tea rooms and TV studios. After a dull evidence-taking session on Monday, there was a fruitful informal briefing with Lord (Tom) Strathclyde, Leader of the Lords, and his Liberal Democrat deputy Lord (Tom) McNally: both Toms were anxious to hear from me how the committee is progressing and to start thinking about tactics. In this company at least, Strathclyde is robust. This may not be unconnected to the defeat shortly before, when peers (including me – my first rebellion) backed the bishops in sending back a feature of the government's benefits cap which would especially target children.

And at Tuesday Questions he was even more explicit in dismissing the pervasive rumours that the Prime Minister is about to nominate sixty new peers – forty Conservatives, fifteen Liberal Democrats and only five Labour – to rebalance the arithmetic after all the Blair appointments. He said it would be "absurd and seen to be absurd".

Later, a gathering under the auspices of Unlock Democracy offered an opportunity to compare notes with other reformers, notably three key Labour MPs. They don't seem very confident that Ed Miliband, or their shadow Cabinet, will stick to their long-held promise of democratic reform. Since it is increasingly evident that the key to eventual success depends on a good majority in the Commons this is depressing. Playing with the excuse that everything must wait for a referendum is no substitute for consistent leadership.

Waiting for more votes on the Welfare Bill on Wednesday (and a substantial defeat, this time led by Tory grandees), I encountered, separately, Lord (Andrew) Adonis and Sir George Young, both excellent allies. I followed up later in the week with a suggestion that informal discussion – and hopefully agreement across the three parties – on handling the immediate opportunity after the joint committee reports in eight weeks' time could be crucial. In his own words George is happy "to do business with you, as always". As Leader of the Commons he has a proper role in thinking through this process, while Andrew is the leading advocate in the Labour Party. Getting them together, with perhaps a couple of MPs from the committee, could be very timely.

At the same time, in the aftermath of the welfare defeats, the BBC TV *Daily Politics* ran over the Lords reform ground again. I got a brief look-in, but Mark Harper was the undoubted star, as consistent and rational as he was at our Liberal Democrat backbench committee earlier in the week. The strategic choice, he has said, is continual increases in the size of the appointed House – rebalancing after each general election – or democratic reform.

6–10 February: At the joint committee meeting on Monday evening there were two significant developments. First, the opponents of all reform bent the chairman's ear at great length on their desire to record a 'minority report'. Since we reformers are not yet confident that we have a majority this is perversely encouraging. And then we started working through a draft note of the main issues, as identified by the clerks, from which it is apparent that we need more time for 'deliberating'; there was a rearguard attempt to seek a further delay in reporting, but this was firmly squashed by the majority. We will have a couple of extra sessions in March instead.

I arrange a gathering of eight reformer allies – all three parties and the cross-benchers represented – on Wednesday to agree on our 'red lines'. Obviously, we will do everything we can to keep the fully elected versus 80%-elected options in play, in order to snuff out any further attempt at reduction in democratic legitimacy. The other issues are less critical, but we are conscious that we should confine ourselves to the absolute essentials. For example, we agree to try to keep out of the detailed salary arrangements.

Two other side shows are in full swing. Nick Clegg and Mark Harper are wanting careful briefing in advance of their joint appearance on 27 February. The logistics are tricky, all because of some need for the Deputy Prime Minister to be involved in strategic talks about Somalia. My input will have to be at a more mundane level.

Meanwhile, David Steel's very unambitious private member's bill – seen by some as a clever distraction from the government's more radical proposals – is the subject of intense arm-twisting behind the scenes. When it re-emerged into the light of day on Friday he had to drop its only really crucial provision – removing the by-elections by which the ninety-two remaining hereditary peers are replaced by others – in the face of 300 amendments from the diehards. In the debate David put a brave face on his retreat, bemoaning the continuation of this absurd anachronism, but I pointed out that the bill is now 'emasculated'. I was not popular. This must surely end the farcical claim that the Steel Bill could prevent the need for more radical reform: a serious defeat for the proponents of a fully appointed House.

20–26 February: Recess for the Commons last week, but for the Lords now, although it is a mystery why peers' grandchildren are supposed to have a different half-term week from that enjoyed by MPs' children. The suspicion is that the establishment wanted to ski at cheaper rates, and when the latter were not clogging up the slopes.

Neither week is very quiet for me, however. The Cabinet

Office team are in overdrive to prepare a comprehensive brief for the Clegg/Harper appearance before the committee, so copious meetings and messages throughout. I have to desert our own grandchildren in a couple of days to return to Westminster. I arranged to take Andrew Adonis and Laura Sandys to meet George Young, to discuss the dangerous political vacuum into which our committee report will emerge during the Easter recess. Left to themselves, the media will undoubtedly play up the alarmist battle cries of the last-ditch opponents.

Meanwhile, we were not assisted by media appearances by Liberal Democrat President Tim Farron, who opined that a more democratic Lords could have sufficient legitimacy to challenge the primacy of the Commons, and by self-appointed Liberal Democrat gadfly (Lord) Matthew Oakeshott[21], who invented a conspiracy theory equating Conservative anxiety to complete the constituency boundary changes with Liberal Democrat enthusiasm for Lords reform. Both are superbly ill-informed, but nevertheless thought to be speaking on behalf of those of us who are aware of developments. Lord preserve us from our friends!

And on 24 February there was another diversion. The *Daily Mail* ran a story as follows: 'The first elections to a reformed House of Lords will be held in 2015 under dramatic plans drawn up for David Cameron by his stepfather-in-law and other peers . . . Government sources say.' The online version is accompanied by a fetching photo of William Astor dressed in a morning suit for a wedding. A completely misleading account of the current state of play includes the statement 'This idea is being pushed by Viscount Astor and [Liberal Democrat peer] Lord Tyler.' The story implies we are already considering a retreat position – a putative Plan B. I wrote a note to him to say that I have not spoken to the *Daily Mail*, never had any contact with the journalist concerned, and am bemused by this tale. However, *The Guardian* today has a slightly similar report, without the inaccuracies or reference

21 Lord Oakeshott of Seagrove Bay, a former Treasury spokesperson.

to me. A No. 10 spin doctor, spinning out of control?

27 February: Final briefing meeting at noon with Clegg and Harper together. I am again glad I have spent so much time and energy urging that they should appear as a duet, rehearse together and each make a short opening statement, to catch the media before they get bored with long-winded questioning. Nick expressed delight – "the best briefing I have had for any encounter" – and he and I agreed with Mark lines to take on the Farron and Oakeshott red herrings.

When the time came for the committee they both performed most effectively, keeping their cool despite continual provocation. I am so attuned to convoluted, garrulous and opinionated questions from some of our more negative peers that I hardly noticed, but evidently the journalists present were taken by surprise. Even Quentin Letts in Tuesday's *Daily Mail* seems less disposed to defend the status quo after hearing them in action.

It is increasingly obvious (to me, at least) that the biggest obstacle will be the illusory suggestion that a reform bill will dominate the next session to the exclusion of everything else. A group of twenty Conservative peers are reported to be prepared to filibuster and cause trouble for ALL other government legislation, in an effort to postpone and therefore drive the bill out of time. I and others were able to take to the airways to point out that the public – and their MPs – will see this as self-interested obstruction . . . a guaranteed way for the government to win in the Commons, where it really matters.

And both *The Spectator* and the *New Statesman* gathered more positive messages from the week's events, not least that Ed Miliband and the Labour front bench are coming round to appreciate the political dangers of casting themselves alongside the opponents of reform. I took the opportunity to encourage allies like Neil Kinnock, Andrew Adonis and Michael Wills.

2 March: On Friday the chairman's first draft of our report was e-mailed to us, protected by a password, and I am once again dazzled by the sheer ingenuity and professionalism of the clerks, as directed by Ivor Richard. It is an excellent start, but the next three weeks will be a hard slog. Much of a damp weekend was devoted to it.

5–7 March: Before our first onslaught on the draft report in the private committee meeting on Monday evening I phoned as many of the reformer team as possible. We agree to let the opponents nitpick extensively, and try to restrain ourselves to concentrate on the essentials. The committee discussion is tortuous in the extreme, several angels dancing on the top of tiny semantic pins. Thanks to diplomatic (and more succinct) interventions from the younger Conservative MPs we at least agree on ways in which we can record majority views for the purpose of clear recommendations. A smaller gathering of confirmed reforming allies on the Tuesday further crystallised our priorities. We all subscribe to my Liberal Democrat colleague John Thurso's thesis: what really matters are the bold-type recommendations, which will be gathered together in a separate section of the report, since this is what all but the anoraks will read.

Later I found myself right behind William Astor as we emerged from the Division Lobby. We stopped to compare notes. He said he was as embarrassed as I was by the *Daily Mail* 'revelation' a couple of weeks back, because he worried that the PM might think he had spoken out of turn. However, when he mentioned this to 'Dave' the latter appeared to be himself contrite, admitting that he himself might have slipped up, hinting to journalists that a retreat strategy might be needed if the going got too tough. We agree that a Plan B could be sensible – but kept very firmly in a back pocket. But what a curious episode!

Yet another committee meeting on Wednesday morning: Ivor is stepping up the pace, determined to prevent the reactionaries from forcing the whole process out of time. We agreed to two more extra meetings in the following weeks. Gavin Barwell and I both latched on to comments from Lord (David) Trefgarne[22] which appear to support our insistence that the relationship between the two Houses should be allowed to evolve naturally as the reformed Lords becomes more democratically legitimate. Since he is a hereditary peer, and scarcely a rabid revolutionary, his proposed compromise may carry extra weight.

Alex and I have combed through the draft report and submitted some forty corrective and textural amendments to the clerks, who express gratitude. It will be interesting to see how many survive into the next draft. I remain very anxious to avoid artificial and discriminatory distinctions between elected and appointed members of the reformed House: why should all the former be salaried full-timers (assuming their electors want them to retain outside experience) while the latter are assumed to be part-time dilettantes?

12–15 March: The pace is hotting up, with two long joint-committee meetings in the week, interspersed with gatherings of our reformers to agree on tactics. We discussed all the amendments tabled and allocated the lead role to one of our number, to check significance and the need to resist, so none will slip through unnoticed. The two Labour women peers – Lady Symons[23] and Lady Andrews[24] – excel themselves in finding ways to oppose the bill. As soon as they lose or withdraw one foot-dragging suggestion they pop up with another.

By contrast our team have relatively few substantial changes to suggest, because the general thrust of the draft report reflects the majority, positive, view of the bill. Gavin is especially adept at spotting the infelicitous phrase, but his improvements are largely uncontroversial.

The votes come next week.

22 Lord Trefgarne, a former Conservative minister.
23 Baroness Symons of Vernham Dean, a former minister in the Blair government.
24 Baroness Andrews, a former minister in the Blair and Brown governments, and until recently chairperson of English Heritage.

19 March: Got in early for a lengthy session with the allies, almost all of whom packed into a tiny interview room in Portcullis House. Again, the preparatory work by my long-suffering parliamentary assistant, Alex, is paying off, because busy MPs have hardly had time to read all the amendments, let alone appreciate their significance.

When we started work in the joint committee we were soon faced with a strategic vote: do we agree in principle that 'The reformed second chamber of legislature should be elected' or not. The anti-democratic tendency put up a spirited rearguard fight. Gavin, ever the diplomat, suggested a modification which gathered in a waverer, and we just got our majority for a House with an 'electoral mandate'. If I had moved this, I suspect we would have failed: it's the 'good cop, bad cop' routine.

We lost one other vote, however, because a key ally was detained by a delayed hospital appointment. The result is a totally illogical assertion that 'A more assertive House would **not** enhance Parliament's overall role in relation to the activities of the executive.' Lola Young[25] pointed out the absurdity of a conclusion which does not follow from the preceding argument, but it was too late. Our missing extra supporter arrived just a few minutes later, and further votes maintained progress – so much so that the opposition appeared to lose heart. We even steered through the tricky decision to prevent delay of the bill while the refuseniks argued over the future relationship of the two Houses. Lord (Philip) Norton[26] provided surprising support for my case, by tabling an amendment pointing out that before the new elected members have arrived they can scarcely be expected to endorse any agreement on this. Did he mean to help?

By the three-hour mark, despite interruptions for divisions in both Houses, we had achieved some real advance, and the chairman adjourned us.

25 Baroness Young of Hornsey, a cross-bencher.
26 Professor Lord Norton of Louth, a Conservative peer and Professor of Government at Hull.

20 March: Alex and I worked until after 11 p.m. to provide guidance on all the amendments we will face in the morning, reinforced by an e-mail of meticulous comments from Gavin.

21 March: The allies gathered for a short exchange of views before the 9.30 a.m. start of the joint committee. The first key vote on the choice between a fully elected and a mainly elected House put the 'neither' tendency in an agitated quandary, but the chairman was adamant that we must recommend one or the other. This was the moment of truth for those who have been saying, "All or nothing." The 80%-elected option won by 16 votes to 6 – far better than we expected. What happened to the other four committee members?

Similarly we won votes and secured support for non-renewable fifteen-year terms, which the government – building on all the previous cross-party studies – believes to be essential to avoid unnecessary and objectionable rivalry with MPs.

After two hours, when the MPs wanted to get to Prime Minister's Questions and prepare for the budget statement, we had got through six more sections of the draft report. An unexpected triumph for the chairman: his determination to concentrate minds on the big-issue recommendations first, in each section, is paying off.

However, we reassembled for a further hour at 5 p.m. The only major surprise was that John Stevenson[27] persuaded a majority (including Lord (Jeff) Rooker, a former senior minister in the Lords, and me, but not the chairman) that any extra ministers nominated by the Prime Minister should leave once they cease to be ministers and have no vote. Logical but challenging!

As the others dispersed, the chairman and clerks told me that, although we seem on course to finalise the report on Monday, it will be kept under wraps until the two Houses return after the Easter recess, planned for Monday 16 April.

27 Conservative MP for Carlisle.

"Not even the Leader of the Lords will see it before then . . . although the government may have a shrewd idea of what is recommended." I am sure they will.

22 March: A curious twist to this tale: the government Chief Whip announced that our recess will continue for an extra week to Monday 23 April. We have been working hard and late on the Welfare, Health and Legal Aid Bills, so this may be the reason, but the Commons have been marking time. Will they come back on the 16th? The danger is that, in the longer news vacuum, intentionally or unintentionally, the media will pick up the more extreme misconceptions and deliberate misrepresentations of the committee's work. Next week, my efforts to alert allies, outside the committee, to be ready to rebut such nonsense will have to be renewed.

26 March: It was the showdown, the final committee session and a few vital debates and decisions were to come. I had a few phone conversations with allies to ensure we didn't duplicate unnecessarily or allow some dilution of the now reasonably robust set of recommendations to slip past us. After a convoluted discussion of the logic for retaining ex officio seats for a dozen bishops, a vote gave them a reprieve. The only lost vote for the government's position is a 13–8 victory (with some abstentions) for those who judge the issue to merit a post-legislative referendum: since this was Labour's position in the 2010 general election, and it appeals to all who will stop at nothing to try to stop reform, the majority represent a curious alliance of reformers and reactionaries. I am willing to bet that this recommendation will be leaked within the week.

The chairman took us all off for a celebratory drink. After thirty meetings, interminable evidence and some knife-edge votes this must be one of the most intensive pre-legislative scrutiny processes ever.

27 March – 16 April: During the Easter recess there were indeed some self-serving leaks. One journalist told me of a detailed brief from a Labour source. Other correspondents dug discriminatorily to suit their editorial prejudices, with some very misleading results. As I anticipated, the referendum issue caused some concern in the Cabinet Office. I observed that it might be difficult for opponents of reform, in both Houses, to argue, at one and the same time, that the public must decide, but in the meantime they want to kill the bill. That won't prevent them from trying it on.

Our conversations turned to cross-party efforts to secure some media appreciation of the general thrust of the committee report when it is published on 23 April. MPs are back during the week beginning 16 April, but we peers are still away, in my case working hard at home. Innumerable phone conversations: can I agree a *Guardian* scene-setting piece with Andrew Adonis for that Monday morning, not breaking the embargo on the report but demonstrating that the status quo is not a viable option? In any case, resistance to reform may simply bolster support for abolition. Already, more people favour sweeping away the second chamber altogether than retaining a fully appointed House.

In addition, the four reformer Conservative MPs on the committee will encourage their backbench colleagues to take a positive position on the proposals, while Labour MP allies will do the same on their side. And we are arranging for a cross-section of committee members to offer a briefing to selected journalists after the chairman's press conference on Monday morning.

My carefully arranged phone conversation with Mark Harper, to exchange ideas about the way forward, eventually took place after a 10 p.m. division in the Commons. He is such a very articulate and committed advocate for the reform package, and I didn't want either to miss out on his advice or to fail to share our plans with him. He is bloodied but unbowed by an encounter with the 1922 Committee.

During the weekend immediately before publication day rumours abound. I used the excuse of mobile inaccessibility in deepest Cornwall (where we are walking with friends and celebrating the twentieth anniversary of my return to the Commons in April 1992) to avoid any media interviews. Despite frantic texts from Paddy Ashdown ("We're letting the reactionaries dominate the airwaves") I eventually persuaded him and our party press office that we should leave the internal wrangling in the Conservative Party on this issue to them: emerging with all guns firing (the Ashdown strategy) would only reinforce the impression that this is a Clegg/Liberal obsession rather than coalition government policy.

23 April: Publication day at last, with the product of thirty committee meetings and interminable discussion out in the open at last. As I stepped off the train at Paddington I was hailed by Mark Harper, arriving from his constituency in the Forest of Dean, so we shared our plans and prognoses for the day on the Tube to Westminster. As I arrived in the office we got the first firm indication of the line the opponents of reform from the committee were going to take – although they included every conceivable favoured alternative to serious reform, they seem able to agree that the government's proposals, now broadly endorsed by the majority on the committee, will cost a lot of money. We are forewarned.

Chairman Ivor Richard launched the report at 11 a.m., and a cross-party selection of reformers (Gavin Barwell, Ann Coffey, Laura Sandys, John Stevenson, Malcolm Wicks[28], Lola Young and I) presented the case for at 11.40. Some of the 'Alternative Report' authors, led by Gillian Shepherd[29], Liz Symons and Peter Hennessy, retaliated at noon. It was very noticeable that the proponents tend to be from the Commons end of the building while the opponents occupy the red leather last ditches at the other end.

Throughout the day I was pursued by media invitations, but especially for BBC TV *Newsnight*. They were cagey about the

28 Late Labour MP for Croydon North.
29 Baroness Shepherd of Northwold, former Conservative Education Secretary.

format and other participants. In the end I was relieved to be upstaged by Mark, because we were to be in the midst of 'ping-pong' on the Legal Aid Bill in the Lords, with frequent knife-edge votes. I was still in the office, waiting for yet more possible divisions, when I watched Mark tangle with David Steel. It would have been incredibly embarrassing for me to have had to tell a very old friend and colleague that he was talking complete nonsense and misquoting the recommendations of the report, but Mark did it with his usual charm. How David squares his long-standing commitment to a fully elected House with the excuses for inaction he keeps handing to the 'not at any price' refuseniks is quite beyond me.

The rest of the week was characterised by intermittent skirmishes: exchanges in the chamber (in which I observe that nobody seemed to be analysing the risks of NOT reforming its composition) and media obsession with those hair-raising but wildly exaggerated estimates of cost. These will have to be the two areas for special attention for my speech in the debate on Monday. Alex and I attempted some coordination of the contributions from other Liberal Democrats. As the week wore on, the number of speakers on the list grew to sixty-five, and Tom Strathclyde gave in to those (mostly on the Labour benches) who don't want to stay up late into the night to hear the wind-up speeches, and he decreed that we could start again on Tuesday morning.

Meanwhile Paddy and I – independently – came to the conclusion that we Liberal Democrats (and Nick Clegg in particular) need to relax at this stage on the option of a post-legislative referendum. We should be on the side of public involvement. If there is a clear public demand to have the last word, and especially if the current peers are obstructing the will of the majority of MPs, then they should be able to trigger a referendum, perhaps by means of an e-petition.

In any case, Cameron and No. 10 are much more vulnerable. How can they resist a referendum on exit from Europe, for which there is so much more public insistence, if they promote one for Lords reform? And how would Labour and Miliband explain opposition to the bill in the Commons if they were granted their wish of public confirmation? It would remove their fig-leaf logic for obstruction and reveal their deep divisions.

30 April – 1 May: Peers engaged in their favourite hobby – navel-gazing. From 3 p.m. until after midnight (with forty minutes taken out for the apparently less important issue of the government's courtship of Rupert Murdoch) some sixty-five members insisted on repeating their views on the reform of their precious chamber.

Ostensibly, this was a debate to take note of the report of the joint committee, but few contributions demonstrated that it has been read, let alone understood.

Introducing the debate Ivor Richard emphasised that the committee had agreed that "The reformed second chamber should have an electoral mandate" by a clear majority. He said, "Of the thirteen in favour, nine were MPs and four were peers. Of the non-contents, seven were peers, one was an MP and one was the Right Reverend Prelate the Bishop of Leicester." He explained that the 80:20 split of elected to appointed members, the voting system, the single fifteen-year terms and the transitional arrangements were all recommended on a unanimous or majority vote, many of them by a substantial margin.

Downhill from then on: the Leader of the Opposition (Baroness Jan Royall) is shameless in what one of her flock later described to me as 'unprincipled opportunism'. Most of those who spoke from the Labour benches followed her lead, with only a very few sticking to their previous convictions and principles (Lords Brooke, Campbell-Savours, Desai, Dubs, Hoyle, Witty and the Baronesses Morgan, Kennedy and Whitaker). True to form the Conservatives are more uniformly antagonistic to change, but two speeches from younger peers were both more analytical and more favourable – from Lord Bates and Lord True. By 7 to 3 the Liberal Democrats support the joint committee, although Paddy Ashdown rather spoiled our chances of positioning the bill as a combined, united coalition initiative by leading the charge on all comers with his customary Liberal gusto.

By midnight very few of us were left (I was the only surviving committee member for the last hour). Peers may rejoice in the quality of our debates, and the vital role we play in the nation's affairs, but not after the dinner hour. Because Tom Strathclyde's deal with Labour transferred the final stages to the next morning these dilettantes were not obliged to stay up into the small hours.

I got my chance to speak up for the committee later in the morning. The Labour benches don't like being reminded of their past promises, and they had a sustained go at me, while the Conservatives seemed happy for me to take the brunt of the attack. At least the wild scaremongering on cost has been challenged by reference to the committee's report. A number of hitherto silent reformers made a point of congratulating us on our stand afterwards.

Perhaps the last word from Ivor Richard sums it all up: "I have always been in favour of what the late John Smith used to call a predominantly but not exclusively elected House of Lords. If the Labour Party's position has now changed, I would be upset."

I suspect that there are many more upsets to come.

* * * * *

A few months later, on 11 July 2012, the House of Commons gave the government's bill, on which our committee had lavished so much scrutiny, a record majority for its second reading of 338 votes.

Perhaps even more significantly there was a very substantial majority of supporting MPs in all three major parties: 193 to 89 Conservatives, 202 to 26 Labour and 53 to nil Liberal Democrats.

However, since the Labour leadership refused to support a

programme motion – any programme motion – to manage the parliamentary time spent on the bill, my old ally Sir George Young had to announce that there could be no immediate progress. David Cameron undertook to try to persuade his colleagues to press on, but when he failed Nick Clegg pulled the bill. Had Labour not sacrificed their principles and manifesto promises on the altar of expediency, there might have been – by the end of the 2012/2013 session – a Reform Act, or at least the likelihood of one achieved through use of the 1911 and 1949 Parliament Acts.

Don't Fall Asleep.

THE ONE-WOMAN COMMITTEE

It was May 1985 when we reached the decisive lap of the race to choose the Channel-crossing link. Ministers had reduced the runners to four, of which the solution promoted by the Channel Tunnel Group was the only one to rely on a rail link in a tunnel, the others all favouring a variety of road-based bridges and tunnels. As the director responsible for public policy in the Good Relations Group, a London consultancy led by the redoubtable Tony Good, I was part of the team advising this Anglo-French consortium.

The other three candidates all played to the motorist lobby. Eurobridge proposed a vast suspension bridge, with the roadway protected from the weather in a giant tube. Euroroute involved a thirteen-mile road tunnel, between two artificial islands, approached by two bridges. Channel Expressway came up with large-diameter road tunnels with mid-Channel ventilation.

Our chairman was Sir Nicholas Henderson, a charming, eloquent and distinguished-looking diplomat of the old school, former Ambassador to Paris and Washington. As the fateful decision approached, a personal invitation to No. 10 loomed. We spent two days at the company offices in Suffolk Street, off Trafalgar Square, carefully briefing him for every conceivable question. I recall the comprehensive technical case marshalled by Tony Gueterbock (later to inherit the title of Lord Berkeley, sitting opposite me in the Lords as a Labour peer) who was, and is, a formidable transport expert. He was able to demonstrate that, since rail freight only became economic if it travelled more than 400 kilometres, linkage to the Continental network alone could return it to profitability. The advantages, not least to the environment, were self-evident. Henderson took copious notes, in a rather battered notebook and with what looked like a code of his own invention. The briefing sessions lasted for some hours, but – as a consummate professional – he seemed to take it all in his stride.

The decisive interview took place on 13 May. To the accompaniment of martial music from Horse Guards Parade, where a rehearsal for Trooping the Colour was taking place, Sir Nicholas apparently battled valiantly, fully aware that the road-bridge option was the current favourite.

When he returned later that day he was clearly in need of a stiff drink. Our inner group from the consultancy were agog.

He told us that "Mrs Thatcher was very charming, as always. How did I take my coffee? No sugar, of course? But milk? A little chat about the old days in Paris. I set out the stall, but I knew that she thought railways to be dirty things of the past, to be swept away by good housekeeping, and that she never travelled by rail. When I explained the particular characteristics of our scheme, and its merits compared with our rivals, her eyes glazed over. I deployed our 'rolling road' idea, but even that didn't seem to do the trick. I knew it was time for my coup de grâce. I leant forward and said, 'Prime Minister, many heads of government, and indeed heads of state, have been called upon to cut ribbons to open great bridges, linking areas, even countries, together. Imagine the experience of those who – after a century of failure – drive the first train under the Channel.' Her eyes lit up – she has remarkable eyes, as you know – and she said,

'Nicko, you have a point.' I came away soon after."

Some weeks later we learnt that we were the government's favourite option, but it was not until the following January that the decision was announced. Just recently I heard from a peer who was a senior member of Mrs Thatcher's Cabinet that they were taken by surprise when the Prime Minister and her Secretary of State for Transport, Nicholas Ridley, finally revealed their preference for the tunnel.

In a recent BBC documentary Norman Fowler – who had been the Secretary of State for Transport earlier in the Thatcher premiership – expressed some bafflement at her choice of the rail option. He gave authoritative endorsement to the widespread impression that she couldn't abide trains, having tussled with the British Rail chairman Peter Parker over the level of government subsidy for the then nationalised network and services. He felt he could explain her support for the overall Channel-crossing concept because she had earlier accepted its feasibility on the assumption that it would be entirely financed by private funding. But why back the one-rail bid?

As a process for achieving decisive action the single-member committee may have its advocates, but (in Britain at least) it is the exception rather than the rule, and requires exceptional circumstances.

Of course, when in May 1994 the rail-based Channel Tunnel opened, Margaret Thatcher had been replaced by John Major. I don't think anyone suggested that he should be allowed to drive a train.

LESSONS LEARNT

Edgar Anstey writes:

In this chapter, meetings are considered from the point of view of an individual member who wishes to influence and persuade people to take the particular decision that he favours. To such a person, the influencing of other people through personal contact is the whole raison d'etre of a committee meeting, since his business might otherwise be settled equally well and more economically of time by exchange of correspondence or telephone calls. He must remember that people are not wholly or even mainly rational in thought or outlook. The mere orderly presentation of facts whether in a paper or at a meeting is not enough. His first endeavour, when introducing his case, should be to win his colleagues' assent that the item is worth discussing at all and sympathy with the line he is taking. Then he must seek to secure not only their agreement that his arguments are sound but their co-operation in getting appropriate action taken in consequence. To have any chance of fulfilling these aims, he must obviously get to know his fellow committee members as people. The question then arises whether to do anything more than this is legitimate, desirable or expedient. Opinions differ, but the general view seems to be that the best 'tactics' are well worth careful consideration. Bearing in mind that tactics, once they are apparent, are often self-defeating.

Committees, p.74

'We learn wisdom from failure much more than from success,' wrote Samuel Smiles. I think I prefer Max Beerbohm's maxim: 'There is much to be said for failure. It is more interesting than success.'

I wish I had come upon Edgar Anstey's advice earlier in my career in public life: I might have avoided several decision-making defeats. However, I think that the lessons I have learnt from failures match much of his recommendations.

For example, solid and imaginative preparation is essential for success. As has been so often apparent this may be the crucial role of a good chairman, underlining the importance of his or her selection.

Although I only encountered Edgar's professional guidance much later, I did have early apprenticeship in meeting management from apparently natural masters of the art in Cornwall and Devon.

At the annual meeting of a Cornish village association I witnessed at close hand what seemed to be an effortless example. A newcomer to the parish from 'upcountry' (i.e. England) was full of enthusiasm, ambition and ill-disguised contempt for the seemingly slow pace of all activity. He attended this meeting fully intending to supplant the chairman, or at least obtain one of the key offices to promote his objectives. The incumbent chairman, a wise or to those who did not know him well just a very straightforward local farmer, summed up the situation neatly. He quietly proposed at the outset that, since they were all anxious to build up support in the area, the agenda should be reversed and the first priority should be to elect an enthusiastic 'membership secretary': perhaps the newcomer would like to put his name forward?

The latter demurred: he was so busy settling into the parish, and wouldn't have time to do justice to the role (he had his eyes on a bigger, more glamorous prize). The election of officers continued. When it came to the post of chairman the incumbent expressed his disappointment that the newcomer was too busy to take on the necessary responsibilities, and he was himself re-elected without dissent. So simple, so neat and

I don't think anyone else in the room but me even noticed the sleight of hand.

I must have been extraordinarily fortunate in the happy accident of my training ground: the people of Cornwall and Devon share with other far-flung UK communities (for example, the Scottish Highlands, rural Wales and the remoter parts of Cumbria and Northumberland) something like an inherent talent for steering the decision-making process.

Planning the pace of the programme, arranging the sequence of decisions for maximum progress, and then achieving the elusive but essential balance between directing and gently steering discussion is the art of effective chairmanship.

Ivor Richard, in the Joint Committee on Lords Reform, even managed this combination while appearing to be so laid-back that the casual observer surely suspected no such forethought or sense of direction.

In that case, as so often, the first hurdle was to prevent the opposition from stretching the whole process into irrelevance. They tried all tricks of the committee trade, conscious that sufficient delay would make legislation in that Parliament virtually impossible. The combination of the crafty chairman and clerks, supported by our reform alliance, all determined to avoid wasting time, achieved firm timetabling.

Next we had to secure the overall objective. A tactful and tactical revision of the initial statement of intent to read, "*The reformed chamber of the legislature should have an elected mandate*" secured a 13:9 vote of support – with nine MPs in favour and only one against. That was a crucial factor when we allies published our guide before the Commons debate[1], recommending a positive vote at the second reading.

The third major challenge was the interminable argument that nothing could or should be done to modernise the composition of the Lords until there had been a complete review and reshaping of its relationship with the Commons.

1   *Lords Reform: A Guide for MPs* (published by Gavin Barwell, Ann Coffey, Daniel Poulter, Laura Sandys, Ros Scott, John Stevenson, John Thurso, Paul Tyler, Malcolm Wicks and Lola Young), July 2012.

This argument will be familiar to any member of a committee charged with looking at possible changes: it is the deceptive doctrine of 'unripe time'. Fortuitously, in this case it was demolished by the impeccable logic of Professor Lord Norton of Louth. His statement that agreement on such a changed relationship would be worthless until the new members of the reformed House were in place to endorse it was irrefutable. It meant that we recommended that 'There would be little point in finalising a concordat [between the Houses] to which elected members of the second chamber were not party.' Lord Norton had previously given some intellectual rigour to the refuseniks' arguments, but following his intervention we heard no more of this gambit. Edgar Anstey would have been appreciative of our use of the more persuasive contributions of our opponents.

In parliamentary committees, as in all other walks of life, the preparation process is all-important, and the chairman and clerks can make or break progress. That early lesson of the significance of the agenda has remained with me for nearly fifty years. I have learnt to prepare more thoroughly myself, whatever my role. All those hours thinking through the next steps of the joint-committee discussions, working with others across parties to ensure a coordinated approach, and innumerable conversations with Mark Harper, paid off.

Edgar Anstey's tactical advice about getting to know other committee members, and preparing them to deploy key arguments, proved especially powerful (although I like to think that I had reached this conclusion independently and had employed a similar technique before reading his book!). For example, encouraging the four younger and newer Conservative MPs to take the lead on such issues as the electoral system for the reformed Lords (on which I would have been suspected of being a Liberal fanatic) proved just as successful as when Robin Cook converted Ken Clarke on the same issue.

Similarly, we almost subconsciously moved the joint committee to reject the government's original plan for a House of '300 full-time Parliamentarians' in favour of one of 450, some of whom, whether elected or appointed, could continue in other walks of life, so bringing much needed topical experience and expertise to Parliament. What this would also guarantee would be bigger multi-member constituencies, with a better chance of wider representation in terms of gender, age, ethnicity and social and economic background, as well as party. But the initial thrust of our argument was the workload of the House, and avoiding the trap of more full-time party politicians. Devious? Surely not! But it was certainly a logical path to obtain the support of otherwise hesitant followers.

I must confess too that I was only too delighted when the Conservatives later thought they had won a great tactical victory by forcing the Liberal Democrats to accept an 'open list' electoral system rather than the single transferable vote (STV). Pragmatically, I judge that this system has as many advantages for this particular purpose, but – if they choose to see us reluctantly conceding defeat – so be it: Edgar Anstey would have been proud of us.

But given the subsequent collapse of that bill, what did all those many hours in the joint committee actually achieve? The committee's majority endorsement of the basic principles of the coalition Cabinet's proposals (building on those of the Jack Straw White Paper of 2008) helped secure a record majority in the Commons. This strong in-principle endorsement means that the bill will probably be resurrected after the 2015 election, whatever the party composition of the new government. So they were not, I hope, entirely pyrrhic victories.

John Pardoe once suggested to me that an individual's political success depends on wisdom, skill, perseverance, powers of persuasion . . . but above all on luck. Harold Macmillan's emphasis on the overwhelming impact of events carried a similar message. Just imagine Eden without Suez, Thatcher without the Falklands, Blair without Iraq, or even Cameron without Syria.

If there is one critical element of the decision-making

process to which both Edgar Anstey and I may have given insufficient attention it is the timescale. In the joint committee, success was contingent on brisk progress. In other situations, it can be dependent on a willingness to take a bit more time, even if there is an outside clamour for instant answers.

Looking back at the coalition negotiations of May 2010 some participants (and many observers) have regretted the speed with which they were conducted. In particular, denied the cumbersome but comprehensive consultation offered to Liberal Democrat parliamentarians and members, their Conservative opposite numbers have complained that they were 'bounced' or 'faced with a fait accompli', as a result of the need for speed. This is unfair and unreasonable on two grounds. David Cameron was then operating on the common assumption that each day's delay risked a deepening financial crisis, with a run on the pound.

Much of the media had fallen for the dire warnings of the rapid right: on eve of poll the *Daily Mail* had forecast economic and social disaster under the headline **'PARALYSED BRITAIN! BEFORE CASTING YOUR VOTE, READ THIS NIGHTMARE ACCOUNT OF THE LAST TIME WE HAD A HUNG PARLIAMENT – AND THE CHILLING PARALLELS WITH TODAY'**. The article was accompanied by hair-raising photos of riots in Greece. Although other commentators tended to discount this paper's 'increasingly apocalyptic visions should Britain fail to elect a majority government'[2], some more serious papers joined in the chorus urging a rapid conclusion to the inter-party talks. Cameron may have seen this as an opportunity to force the pace with his colleagues.

On the other hand, Nick Clegg and his negotiating colleagues did manage a sustained and substantial dialogue with key members of his party, despite the constraints of time. It was scarcely Cameron's fault that his party was so totally unprepared in both its mindset and mechanics for such a situation.

2   P. Cowley and D. Kavanagh, *The British General Election 2010* (Basingstoke: Palgrave Macmillan, 2010).

I have no doubt that – if the parliamentary arithmetic is in any way similar in May 2015 – all the leaders and all their parties will benefit from the lessons of 2010. While the circumstances clearly will be different from those of European neighbours who often take weeks or even months to secure coalition agreements, UK politicians (and political commentators) will do well to get some sleep after an exhausting election campaign, before throwing themselves into complicated negotiations. As we now know, the sky does not fall in if the next inhabitant of No. 10 is not identified for a few days. And, after five years of coalition, it will be difficult anyway for the media to represent the absence of a majority government in such blood-curdling terms.

And then there is that vital ingredient, implicit in everything the professional psychologist Anstey identifies in his book: humanity.

"Human nature is very prevalent" a RIBA president once observed to me. We may not need to go as far as Nicko Henderson, faced with the very human frailties of Prime Minister Thatcher, to achieve our decision-making objectives. But the coalition negotiations, and the joint committee alike, all relied on a good measure of human empathy and interaction. Subsequent accounts suggest it was on this key point that Gordon Brown failed to stay in No. 10. Every committee, every opportunity to make a decision, right or wrong, brings together individuals whose prejudices, enthusiasms and self-confidence are in play. That is the challenge.

If I have learnt one lesson, above all, from Edgar Anstey's analysis as well as from my own practical experience of some fifty years of seeking decisions in British public life, it is this: if you ignore human nature, you might as well stay at home.

Do not overdo The Hospitality.

LAST WORD FROM EDGAR ANSTEY

Some people, on the other hand, with no craving for power, become inveigled into joining several committees through a combination of sense of duty and inability to say NO. They find themselves drawn into a seemingly endless round of meetings, in much the same way that other people become entangled in hire purchase repayments. No sooner has one committee finished its work than they become involved in another.

For meetings to seem a burden rather than a pleasure should be taken by the person concerned as a warning signal that he has perhaps joined too many committees and should take stock of the position, concentrating on those in which he is really interested and seeking an opportunity to retire gracefully from any others. Like all good resolutions, however, this may be more easily taken than carried out.

Committees, p.25

The Enticement
of the Forbidden

Protecting Your Marriage

Personal Study and Discussion Guide

Judy Starr

The Enticement of the Forbidden
Protecting Your Marriage
Personal Study and Discussion Guide

Published by
LifeConneXions
A ministry of Campus Crusade for Christ
375 Highway 74 South, Suite A
Peachtree City, GA 30269

Cover by Larry Smith and Associates
Printed in the United States of America
ISBN 1-56399-221-3

Unless otherwise indicated, Scripture quotations are from the *New American Standard Bible*, ©1960, 1962, 1963, 1968, 1971, 1972, 1973, 1975, 1977, 1995 by the Lockman Foundation, La Habra, California.

Scripture quotations designated NIV are from the *New International Version*, © 1973, 1978, 1984 by the International Bible Society. Published by Zondervan Bible Publishers, Grand Rapids, Michigan.

Scripture quotations designated TLB are from *The Living Bible*, © 1971 by Tyndale House Publishers, Wheaton, Illinois.

Contents

This study guide is dedicated to my precious Mom, Dottie Antosh

Mom, you are perfectly described in Matthew 5:6: "Blessed are those who hunger and thirst for righteousness, for they shall be satisfied." What a privilege to have a mother who passionately thirsts for God and His Word. I am indeed blessed. I love you so much!

The Transformation Process

A s I looked down at my wedding ring, my heart ached to be with the man I thought I loved—but he wasn't my husband! So with my heart feeling raw and broken, I chose to leave this man and return home. At that point a hardened, insensitive spirit toward God lay cold inside my soul. But in my desperation to know His presence and peace once again, I determined to hang in there and do whatever it took to soften my hardened heart of stone into a heart of flesh (Ezekiel 11:19). And as I started choosing obedience, God graciously began to tenderize and remold my heart and mind again. I won't tell you it was easy, because that process often felt quite painful! But the end results were worth every moment of the pain required in order to restore my relationship with God and with my husband.

Change is never easy. Yet without change, nothing will grow. Unless the ground is plowed up and overturned, the soil can never be ready to produce crops. The same is true for our lives. Unless we are willing to look into our hearts and overturn those hard, unbroken areas, we will remain in the same ruts and destructive patterns the rest of our earthly days. And the longer we stay that way, the harder it becomes to change!

I still have moments during my time in God's presence when He points His finger at an area in my life that needs changing. When that happens, I often feel tempted to get up and end my time with Him early. But I choose to stay and confront those areas because I know that as I do, He will transform my life and root out the places that need changing so that I can continue to grow.

Although our lives and the world around us constantly change, God and His Word never do. Isaiah writes, *"The grass withers, the flower fades, but the word of our God stands forever"* (Isaiah 40:8). What a blessing to have a Rock upon which we can depend completely, without fail. *"The Rock! His work is perfect, for all His ways are just; a God of faithfulness and without injustice, righteous and upright is He"* (Deuteronomy 32:4). *"The Lord is my rock and my fortress and my deliverer, my God, my rock, in whom I take refuge"* (Psalm 18:2).

Because God and His Word never change, He alone must form the foundation for all we think, believe, and do. That's why you will find so much Scripture throughout *The Enticement of the Forbidden*, and why we will spend time learning from His Word in this study guide. If God said it, it's true, and I'm going to stake my life on it!

For God to truly transform our lives, we must confront our propensity to sin and acknowledge that we can all fall into any sin known to man. That knowledge drives us to come to the Lord each day. It was only when I started coming to the Lord in desperation every morning that I began to witness the miraculous changes in my heart that only He can make. He also began opening my eyes to things in His Word that now form the truths you will read about as you go through *The Enticement of the Forbidden* and this accompanying Personal Study and Discussion Guide. I believe in these truths with all my heart because I have seen in my life and in others' lives the transformation that comes when we follow His Word.

So let's begin this lifelong journey with the Lord by laying a solid foundation so that our lives will become more and more like Christ, shining with His holiness, radiating *"the peace of God, which surpasses all comprehension"* (Philippians 4:7). Such a life is only found in Him!

Using this Study

Thank goodness God didn't create us and then leave us to stumble through life alone! He loves to meet with us and yearns to guide us with His wisdom so that we can become more and more like Christ.

But there are no shortcuts to spiritual growth. That's why I'm excited that you are using this study guide along with reading the book. This daily study will help you apply the truths that you are learning from *The Enticement of the Forbidden* into your own life and marriage. As you dig into His Word and allow Him to transform you, a depth of spiritual life you never dreamed possible will begin to take place. *"For I am confident of this very thing, that He who began a good work in you will perfect it until the day of Christ Jesus"* (Philippians 1:6).

This study can be used in two ways. First, as a personal, daily study, it will help you apply the concepts from *The Enticement of the Forbidden* to your own life, guiding you as you grow deeper in God's Word and protect your marriage. Second, this study guide can also be used with a small group of women. In the back of this book are discussion questions that correspond with each week's lessons. Your discussion group will meet once a week to discuss what you have been learning. However, your answers in the Personal Study will only be addressed in a general sense, so please open your heart honestly before the Lord as you answer the daily questions.

Plan to do these daily lessons during the week, and bring what you have learned to the weekly discussion group. If you do not plan to meet with a discussion group, consider adapting the Discussion Guide as a conversation between you and your accountability partner. If you will not be meeting with anyone, then turn to the Discussion Guide at the end of each week's lessons and go through the questions and material on your own. There is new material in the Discussion Guide that you definitely won't want to miss!

The Personal Study

The Personal Study plan includes five lessons per week. Study one lesson per day, either during your Quiet Time with God or at another time during the day when you can focus on God's Word.

Each daily lesson includes several parts. They are designed to help you focus on God, learn what the Bible says on the subject covered, and apply the truths to your life. These are the lesson components:

Reading

This is the chapter(s) in *The Enticement of the Forbidden* covered in the lesson. Be sure you have read these pages in the book before you work on the lesson. If you read the chapter at an earlier time, reviewing it would be helpful before you prepare to do the lesson.

Spending Time with God

This is a short devotional time that will help you focus on God before you start your lesson.

Evaluating My Views

These questions will help you consider your current views on the topic to be studied. It is essential to be honest about your opinions so that you can address any changes the Lord may want you to make.

Finding God's Perspective

This section will guide you into the Scriptures to help you see what God says about the topic. This is the heart of your study. There's nothing better than digging into His Word!

Checking My Heart

This part of the lesson takes what God says and helps you apply the principles specifically to your unique situation. This is where you examine your heart concerning the issues raised and look at how God may desire you to change.

Allowing God to Transform Me

After learning what God says about the subject and how that affects your life, it's time to implement the principles you have learned. This section is where your study allows God to begin transforming your life.

As you work through the lessons, keep a prayer list in your study guide. You could use the inside front cover to record your requests, or keep a separate piece of paper in your workbook. This will become a great encouragement as you see God's answers to your prayers. Write down requests, answers to prayer, Scripture references that apply to your prayers, and praises to God. Be sure to date your entries so that you can keep track of when your prayers are answered. A suggestion is to make a chart like this one:

Prayer Request	Date	Prayer Request	Date

If you are also participating in a discussion group, include a section for the prayer requests and praises that come from your time with the women in your study group.

Also, designate a section of your prayer chart for your accountability partnership. (In *The Enticement of the Forbidden*, you will learn about setting up accountability.) Pray for your accountability partner's needs regularly. And don't forget to include a section of prayer requests for your husband!

The Discussion Guide

When you meet once a week with your discussion group, you will talk with other women about what you have been learning from the daily lessons. This will be done by going through questions found in the Discussion Guide. God calls us to learn from one another, so receiving the wisdom, viewpoints, and encouragement of other women is vital to achieving maximum spiritual growth. You will find that these sessions also help you stick with the changes you are making in your marriage relationship and in your commitment to God.

If you are the facilitator for a discussion group, you will find the Discussion Guide toward the end of this book. Each week's discussion includes material for your use in guiding your group time. Study this material before leading each weekly session. Your group members do not need to turn to these pages because you will read the questions and added material to them aloud. As the leader, frequently emphasize that all personal information shared within the group must be held in *strictest confidence* by all other group members. Also, remind the women that they will want to be careful about sharing with others any personal and private matters concerning their husbands. The issue of respecting and honoring one another in our marriage is vital, even if the marriage is a difficult one. Therefore, encourage them to consider talking with their husband and, if possible, receiving his permission beforehand to share such things.

Our precious Lord loves us so much and desires to transform us so that we *"may be filled with the knowledge of His will in all spiritual wisdom and understanding"* (Colossians 1:9). What a privilege we have to study His Word and to know God! And as we allow Him to change us, we then experience His fullness and His peace—something that is very precious to me since I stood on the threshold of marital disaster.

As you go through this study, *"I pray that the eyes of your heart may be enlightened, so that you may know what is the hope of His calling, what are the riches of the glory of His inheritance in the saints, and what is the surpassing greatness of His power toward us who believe"* (Ephesians 1:18,19).

Personal Study
Guide

"Trust in the Lord with all your heart and do not lean on your own understanding. In all your ways acknowledge Him, and He will make your paths straight."
Proverbs 3:5,6

Lesson 1
"We Have a Problem"

Note: These daily lessons are for your eyes only. For group discussion times the Discussion Guide, found in the back of this book, asks a new set of questions. So please be as transparent as possible in answering these daily questions.

Reading: chapters 1 and 2.

Spending Time with God

Oh, the heartache and destruction we can cause in our own life and in the lives of those around us when we choose to live according to our selfish desires! How desperately we need God's wisdom and guidance. Proverbs 3:5,6 says, *"Trust in the Lord with all your heart and do not lean on your own understanding. In all your ways acknowledge Him, and He will make your paths straight."* To begin your time in this study, place your heart in God's hands. Read those verses again, thinking about the instructions we are to follow. Then commit this study time to God. Ask the Lord to guide you as you read His Word.

Evaluating My Views

In the space below, write out your perspective of what your marriage relationship is like right now. Especially make note of any ways that emotional and/or physical infidelity may have touched your marriage.

Finding God's Perspective

1. Read Hebrews 13:4. How are God's standards in marriage different than the world's standards?

2. Read 1 Thessalonians 4:1–5. What directions does God give us concerning moral purity?

3. Christian author and clinical psychologist Dr. Willard Harley calls infidelity "the greatest threat to your marriage."[1] How does this quote apply to the Hebrews 13 and 1 Thessalonian 4 passages and to marriages today?

Checking My Heart

According to *Psychology Today* magazine, "Half the American couples over 40 years of age have experienced extramarital affairs at some point."[2] But it doesn't end there. More and more older women are also choosing to follow their feelings rather than their vows.

1. In what ways can a woman choose to commit emotional infidelity even if she hasn't committed physical infidelity?

2. List areas in your life—work relationships, friendships, neighborhood contacts—that could present opportunities toward developing either emotional or physical ties to another man.

3. What steps could you take to avoid compromising situations?

Allowing God to Transform Me

God loves us so much and wants only that which is for our good. As we choose to follow Him, we begin to see how every area of our lives can reflect His purity, and we also experience His peace. As you begin to delve into this study of *The Enticement of the Forbidden*, ask God to help you become more sensitive to His standards for your marriage. If a situation exists in your life where emotional or physical infidelity may have already become a danger point, ask the Lord to give you His perspective on keeping your marriage pure.

Lesson 2
"God's Perspective on Marriage and Wives"

Reading: chapter 3.

Spending Time with God

God tells us, *"The wise woman builds her house, but the foolish tears it down with her own hands"* (Proverbs 14:1). As you think about this verse, ask God to show you what kind of foundation you have for your "life house." Think through the major decisions you have made over the last week. Was each decision made on the basis of God's Word or on what you thought was right?

Evaluating My Views

1. How would you describe your commitment level to your marriage?

2. Write a paragraph on your views about your role as a wife.

3. How does the world's view on how a wife is to relate to her husband differ from your views? How are they the same?

Finding God's Perspective

Because God loves us so much, He gave us clear instructions on how we are designed to function and live. When we disregard these precepts, problems always develop. Psychologist Dr. James Dobson says, "We are all governed by a moral code that cannot be violated without inevitable consequences."[3]

1. After reading Mark 10:6–9, describe in your own words the bond God wants to see in a marriage.

2. Read Ephesians 5:21–33. Write down God's marriage principles for husbands. Then write down God's marriage principles for wives.

Christian author Susan Foh writes: "Wives are to *submit themselves* (reflexive); their submission is voluntary, self-imposed. It is part of their obedience to the Lord; the Lord is the one who commands it, not the husband."[4]

3. What difference does it make to a marriage when the spouses submit to God first?

Checking My Heart

Mike Mason, in his book *The Mystery of Marriage*, calls marriage "an unrelenting guerrilla warfare against selfishness."[5]

1. On the scale below, mark from 1 to 10 how selfish you think you are in your marriage relationship. Do you frequently think about how your marriage can fulfill you and make you happy, or do you usually act out of self-sacrifice and commitment to your husband?

1 —————————————————— 10
Self-sacrificing   Selfish

2. How does 1 Peter 3:1–4 apply to your relationship with your husband?

3. In what ways can you be an example of Proverbs 31:10–12 in your marriage?

Allowing God to Transform Me

Turn your husband over to God's care. Thank God for your husband's positive characteristics. Now thank Him for your husband's weaknesses and ask God to help you show respect toward your spouse, exhibiting a gentle and quiet spirit.

Lesson 3
"God's Perspective on Affairs and Divorce"

Note: Remember, all these daily lessons are for your eyes only.

Reading: Review chapter 3 from the section titled "God's Perspective on Affairs" to the end.

Spending Time with God

As you read the following verse, ask God to reveal any ways that you may have a casual attitude toward keeping your marriage pure and sacred. Lay those before the Lord and thank Him that He can enable you to change these attitudes or actions. *"Marriage should be honored by all, and the marriage bed kept pure, for God will judge the adulterer and all the sexually immoral"* (Hebrews 13:4, NIV).

Evaluating My Views

1. What kind of emotional response does the phrase "she's having an affair" elicit from you?

2. How do you feel about Charles Colson's statement: "Even under the worst of circumstances—adultery, abuse, and abandonment—God does not command divorce. He merely permits it. And divorce is always a trauma. In this age of no-fault divorce, Christians ought to do everything possible to protect their marriages."[6]

Finding God's Perspective

There is definitely something enticing about the forbidden. Just ask Eve. The one thing she was denied in the midst of paradise—the fruit of the tree—became an alluring temptation. And the results of her choice to disobey God brought disaster (Genesis 3)! Sin will always be tempting. That's why we so desperately need to know *God's* perspective—because He knows the *results* of our choices.

1. How does God describe an immoral woman in Proverbs 5:3–6?

2. According to Proverbs 6:27–29,32, what is the result of a person's choice of adultery?

3. Looking at Malachi 2:16 and Mark 10:9, what does God teach us concerning divorce?

Checking My Heart

1. What are some of the consequences that could occur if you ever decided to divorce?

2. In a study on marriage and divorce, 92 percent of the couples who remained together in spite of serious marital troubles later said they were "glad they were still together."[7] Why do you think they were happier?

Most of us think that because we are Christian our marriage will be "Christian." But a godly marriage doesn't just happen because we go to church and even read our Bibles. It takes work, and it requires building safeguards against the onslaughts that inevitably will occur. We should fear the ease with which we can so easily fall to temptation and sin. God warns us, *"How blessed is the man who fears always, but he who hardens his heart will fall into calamity"* (Proverbs 28:14).

3. What examples can you give from your own experience that show the truth of that verse?

Allowing God to Transform Me

Ask God to give you His perspective on affairs and divorce. If you have feelings of discontent in your marriage, turn those over to God. (He already knows your heart.) Ask Him to help you persevere through troubled times, remembering that He can restore your love.

Lesson 4
"How Can a Christian Woman Fall into Infidelity?"

Reading: chapter 4.

Spending Time with God

Temptation leading away from the Lord always looks exciting and enticing. That's why we're tempted! Yet the result brings only long-term sorrow and destruction. God tells us that we are fools when we enjoy sin. *"A fool finds pleasure in evil conduct, but a man of understanding delights in wisdom"* (Proverbs 10:23, NIV). Examine your heart before God, asking Him to reveal where sin is a pleasure to you. Ask Him to help you desire to be pure and wise in all areas of your life, especially in those that God reveals as impure.

Evaluating My Views

Dr. Shirley Glass says about some spouses: "For them, part of the passion and excitement of an affair is the lying and getting away with something forbidden."[8]

1. In what ways is this like your life?

Dr. Scott Haltzman writes about unfaithful partners: "For an overwhelming majority of spouses who cheat—80 percent—the reason is not sexual. Most simply seek validation, warmth, understanding, or love."[9]

2. Which areas do you feel are most needy in your relationship with your husband? (Check those that apply.)

❑ Need for his respect and validation
❑ Need for warmth and love
❑ Desire for greater understanding
❑ Desire for his attention, to feel important
❑ Need for time alone together
❑ Desire for excitement

3. How does your daily schedule contribute to your pleasure or dissatisfaction with your marriage?

Finding God's Perspective

1. Isaiah 30:1 says, *"'Woe to the rebellious children,' declares the Lord, 'Who execute a plan, but not Mine, and make an alliance, but not of My Spirit, in order to add sin to sin.'"* What is God saying about the person who is determined to do things her way rather than God's way?

2. Rewrite Proverbs 9:13–18, putting the situation into a modern setting.

3. How can Psalm 20:1–5 give you hope for how God will help you overcome any difficulties you are having in your marriage or your life?

Checking My Heart

Attraction to another man can happen to anyone at any age. This infatuation most often begins with someone who meets your desires for warmth, validation, and love. Your self-image receives strokes—someone finds you attractive and desirable! Suddenly, you experience feelings you don't want to lose. There is a sense of freshness in the excitement of this secret infatuation.

1. In what ways have you found this to be true in your life?

2. What steps will you take to avoid situations in which you are prone to temptation in this area?

Allowing God to Transform Me

Read Psalm 1:1–3 *"How blessed is the man who does not walk in the counsel of the wicked, nor stand in the path of sinners, nor sit in the seat of scoffers! But his delight is in the law of the Lord, and in His law he meditates day and night. He will be like a tree firmly planted by streams of water, which yields its fruit in its season and its leaf does not wither; and in whatever he does, he prospers."* Seeing how easily choices of sin can snowball, ask God to continue revealing your heart. He is the only One who can give you the power to change. Ask Him to help you follow His path and to delight in His wisdom.

Lesson 5
"Opportunities Everywhere"

Reading: Glance back through the main headings in chapters 1–4.

Spending Time with God

God listens to those who truly turn to Him. Read Psalm 51:1-10. Tell God how David's feelings reflect your own. Let God know how sorry you are for any indiscretions you may have committed against your husband. Ask Him to give you a clean heart and a steadfast spirit.

Evaluating My Views

1. How have your opinions about infidelity changed since you began this study?

2. How do you think our culture has influenced you to hold wrong views about marriage and unfaithfulness?

3. In what ways could these wrong views lead to disastrous consequences?

Finding God's Perspective

1. Read Colossians 3:12–15. How can you apply these verses to your relationship with your husband?

2. Now go on to read verses 16,17 of Colossians 3. What principles can you take from these verses that can help you manage any difficulties in your marriage or help to strengthen your marriage?

Checking My Heart

1. Look in the book at the scenario that led me (Judy) to attraction toward Eric. (It's found in the beginning of chapter 4 up to the heading "How Women Get Into Problems.") What choices did I make that allowed me to get to the point of falling for another man?

2. Did you see yourself in any of the marriage scenarios described in chapter 4 in the section titled "How Women Get Into Problems"? Describe the similarities.

3. Describe the process you will undertake to make your choices more godly and supportive to your marriage.

Allowing God to Transform Me

Spend time asking God to help you make the choices you listed above.

Note: If you will *not* be meeting with a discussion group or with another person to go through the Discussion Guide, please turn now to page 118 and go through the questions and new material for Week One as if it were another daily lesson. You won't want to miss the additional insights found there!

Lesson 1
"The Results of Our Choices"

Note: Remember, all these daily lessons are for your eyes only. For group discussion times the Discussion Guide, found in the back of this book, asks a new set of questions. So please be as transparent as possible in answering these daily questions.

Reading: chapter 5

Spending Time with God

God is so amazingly patient with sinful humans because He loves us so much and desires to lead us out of our foolish ways. Romans 2:4 says, *"Or do you think lightly of the riches of His kindness and tolerance and patience, not knowing that the kindness of God leads you to repentance?"* Think of ways that God has been kind to you. Consider areas such as health, material possessions, family, jobs, Christian friends, and church support. Thank God for His kindness toward you.

Evaluating My Views

1. Jesus said, *"These things I speak in the world so that they may have My joy made full in themselves"* (John 17:13).[1] How does it make you feel to know that God desires for you to experience an abundant life full of peace and joy?

2. The ability to leave sin and to change your actions (repentance) is a gift from God. How does this make you feel about choices you may be making to continue disobeying Him?[2]

When we choose to continue in sin (disobedience to God) and refuse to change our ways, our conscience can become hardened to God's will until we no longer even hear His voice. And we will reap the full consequences of our actions.

3. Proverbs 29:1 says, *"A man who hardens his neck after much reproof will suddenly be broken beyond remedy."* How could that principle apply to a woman who refuses to follow God's instructions to flee immorality?

Finding God's Perspective

The bottom line for infidelity—or *any* sin—always comes back to the choices we make. And with each choice, we decide whether to follow God or to listen to Satan's temptations. God loves us so much that He sent His Son Jesus to die for us. Satan hates us so much that he wants only that which destroys our lives and our futures. He *wants* our marriages to crumble and our ministries to disintegrate in shame. His desire is to steal and kill and destroy us, and he prowls around like a starving lion awaiting even the smallest opportunity to devour our lives (1 Peter 5:8). He's not called "our adversary" for nothing!

There are only two paths we may follow. In the chart below, contrast the results of choosing Satan's way versus God's way. Think of examples from your life, what you have seen around you, or what you believe may happen.

Verses	Results of Choosing Satan's Way	Results of Choosing God's Way
1 Peter 5:8–10		
John 10:10		
Proverbs 1:28–33		

Checking My Heart

The vows you made on your wedding day were made to God first, then to your husband. Keep this in mind as you answer the following questions.

1. What do you remember about the vows you made to your husband on your wedding day? Write out as much as possible.

2. What do these vows mean to you today? Be honest.

3. We know that God's will for us is always for our good. Read Numbers 30:1,2. How does this verse change your view of your marriage vows?

Allowing God to Transform Me

The Bible tells us to *"offer to God a sacrifice of thanksgiving and pay your vows to the Most High; call upon Me in the day of trouble; I shall rescue you, and you will honor Me"* (Psalm 50:14,15). Call upon God to help you remain true to your marriage vows. Whatever failings you have done are now in the past. Resolve to start anew, keeping your vows sacred from here on.

His Word tells us to offer *"a sacrifice of thanksgiving"* to Him, whether our situation is easy or difficult. Thank Him for your marriage, trusting that He will strengthen you to remain faithful as you call upon Him.

Lesson 2
"Be Honest with Yourself"

Reading: chapter 6.

Spending Time with God

God tells us, *"The heart is more deceitful than all else and is desperately sick; who can understand it? I, the Lord, search the heart, I test the mind, even to give to each man according to his ways, according to the results of his deeds"* (Jeremiah 17:9,10). Ask God to show you what is truly in your heart as you go through this lesson.

Evaluating My Views

1. What do you think of the phrase: "Never underestimate the power of attraction"?

2. How have you seen yourself or someone you know rationalize feelings of attraction toward someone else?

3. How have you witnessed the tendency in human nature to always want more?

Finding God's Perspective

1. One problem we face in our marriage relationships is not being honest with ourselves about our own failings and problems. God's Holy Spirit can help us see ourselves as we truly are. Ask Him to help you in this first step to building a godly marriage: Be honest with yourself.

2. Read Proverbs 12:20. How does this verse apply to emotional and physical infidelity?

3. In Romans 1:21, what process does Paul describe concerning people who keep on sinning?

4. Describe how you can be honest with yourself when confronted with a temptation or an attraction to another man.

Checking My Heart

We can never be truly honest with ourselves until we allow God to reveal those areas in our hearts that may not be readily apparent.

1. List any areas in which you have difficulty with temptation in your marriage. This could include attitudes and thoughts.

2. Read Psalm 5:1–7. What actions do these verses give to help you open your heart to God?

3. Ask God for His perspective on the areas of temptation that you listed in question 1. Then lay those before Him and ask for His strength to resist the enemy and to make godly choices.

Allowing God to Transform Me

Use Psalm 26:2 in a prayer, asking God to continue searching your heart: *"Examine me, O Lord, and try me; test my mind and my heart."* Christ tells us that His grace is sufficient (2 Corinthians 12:9), so ask Christ to strengthen you in your weaknesses. He yearns for us to depend on Him.

Lesson 3
"Be Honest with God"

Reading: In chapter 6, review the section titled "Be Honest with God."

Spending Time with God

Only God can change our perspective to see life through His eyes. Each day, we must let Him rearrange our priorities, make us less selfish, and mold us to be like Christ. This, in turn, *greatly* impacts our marriage. Christian author and speaker Cynthia Heald says, "A wife rightly related to her Lord will be a wife rightly related to her husband."[3]

God tells us that the person with whom He fellowships is the one *"who is humble and contrite of spirit and who trembles at My word"* (Isaiah 66:2). Do you meet with Him each day, understanding that the quality of every single relationship in your life is dependent upon your relationship with God? Take a few moments in prayer to give God first place in your life again.

Evaluating My Views

1. Describe things that cause your heart to become hardened and insensitive to the Lord.

2. Write down the times in your daily schedule when you spend time in God's Word and in His presence.

3. How do you think spending daily, meaningful time in the Bible and in God's presence will keep your spirit tender and sensitive to His leading?

Finding God's Perspective

1. What does Psalm 119:9–11 say are the results of maintaining honesty with God?

2. According to Psalm 119:162–165, what actions keep our heart sensitive to the Lord?

Because I (Judy) believe this with all my heart, let me say it again: I am convinced that *the most critical element in protecting your marriage is your personal time alone with God.* It is irreplaceable; there are no substitutes.

3. In what ways do you need to change your attitude about spending time with the Lord every day?

Checking My Heart

Read Psalm 86:5 to find a wonderful description of God. Because of God's goodness, love, and forgiveness, we can lay all areas of our life at His feet and commit again to maintaining honesty with Him through daily time in His Word and presence.

1. What areas in your life have you kept hidden from the Lord?

2. After studying the verses from Psalm 119 above, what difference will these verses make in your daily schedule so that you can keep a sensitive and tender heart to the Lord?

Allowing God to Transform Me

Read Deuteronomy 10:12,13 and ask God to make this true for your commitment to Him.

Lesson 4
"Be Honest with Your Husband"

Note: Remember, all these daily lessons are for your eyes only.

Reading: In chapter 6, review the sections titled "Be Honest with Your Husband" and "The No Secrets Policy."

Spending Time with God

Godly marriages don't just happen because one Christian marries another Christian. No marriage is without conflicts, trials, and failures in communication. Yet we know that God is committed to seeing our marriage relationship grow and reflect His love. Godly love *"does not rejoice in unrighteousness, but rejoices with the truth"* (1 Corinthians 13:6). Ask God to give you His perspective on how truthfulness in your marriage demonstrates love.

Evaluating My Views

1. Have you ever felt that sudden tingle of attraction toward another man? What did you do with those feelings? Did you follow God's Word or your feelings?

2. If your heart felt drawn toward another man, and you found yourself repeatedly dwelling on thoughts and pictures of the two of you together, would you tell your husband about your fantasies? Why?

3. Dr. Joyce Brothers writes, "When people who are close are not completely honest with each other, certain avenues of intimacy are invariably cut off."[4] Do you think that having a marriage free of deceit and secrets will enhance trust, closeness, and communication? What might change in your relationship if both of you were totally honest?

Finding God's Perspective

Honesty is an incredible protection for Stottler's and my marriage. The moment I sense that Stottler would be unhappy if he knew what I might do, an enormous red flag pops up in my head. Like most of us, if I think I can hide something, I'm far more likely to give it a try. But immediately exposing the temptation causes it to wither and die.

1. God warns us many times in His Word about the consequences of hiding things and being deceitful. Read the following verses, writing down the main idea and consequence of deceitfulness described in each:

   Jeremiah 17:9,10

   Psalm 36:1–3

2. The following verses speak of the benefits of truthfulness. Write down the benefit you receive for being truthful found in each verse:

   Psalm 15:1,2

   Psalm 51:6,7

3. Now compare the two sets of passages. In a sentence, write out why it is so important for you to be truthful with your husband.

Checking My Heart

1. In what areas do I tend to "fudge" the truth or outright lie to my husband?

2. What is my motive for doing this? How does this secrecy affect our marriage?

3. What are some specific steps I can take to begin implementing the No Secrets Policy in my marriage?

Allowing God to Transform Me

In *The Living Bible*, Ephesians 4:15 says, *"We will lovingly follow the truth at all times—speaking truly, dealing truly, living truly—and so become more and more in every way like Christ."* As we have seen in His Word, God repeatedly calls us to honesty in all areas of our life. Pray and ask the Lord to begin making you willing to do *whatever* He calls you to do for the sake of your marriage. He will always give you the strength to obey.

Lesson 5
"Elements of Restoration"

Reading: In chapter 6, review all sections under "Elements of Restoration."

Spending Time with God

After establishing honesty with yourself, with God, and with your husband, you will begin to see changes in your marriage. To allow God's healing and building to continue, ask Him to reveal where your priorities differ from His found in Matthew 22:37. Ask God to give you His wisdom in setting your priorities.

Evaluating My Views

1. Write out a general schedule of your daily activities. Include the time you spend with God (prayer times, reading the Bible, worshiping, ministry), your husband, your family, and work. Can you honestly say that your priorities in life are God first, then your husband, then your children, and finally your ministry and work?

Answer these questions about any improper relationship or fantasy in which you may be involved now, or how you would respond if this were to happen:

2. If you find yourself caught up in romantic or sexual fantasies toward anyone—fictional or real—how are those fantasies affecting your relationship with your husband?

3. If there is another man with whom you've had an improper relationship—either emotionally or physically—what effect has this had on your marriage?

Finding God's Perspective

The Enticement of the Forbidden gives three elements for restoring a damaged marital relationship and for building barriers against future temptations of infidelity. Let's look at God's perspective for each.

1. Cutting off all contact: Read James 1:14,15. How does staying in contact with a person with whom you have an improper relationship fulfill the process in this verse?

2. Set your priorities: Read Proverbs 2:1–12. How does making God and His Word first priority in your life help you keep all your other priorities right?

3. Rebuild trust: Read Philippians 2:3. How does demonstrating a self-sacrificing love that puts your husband above yourself help repair trust in your marriage that you may have damaged through selfish and secret choices?

Checking My Heart

Whether you have been unfaithful emotionally or physically or may have failed to make your marriage the priority it should be, make a plan to begin restoring and protecting your marriage relationship. Write out what you need to do in each of these areas that apply:

1. Cutting off all contact.

2. Setting your priorities.

3. Rebuilding trust.

Allowing God to Transform Me

God tells us, *"Behold, I am the Lord, the God of all flesh; is anything too difficult for Me?"* (Jeremiah 32:27). Thank God that *He* can give you the strength to follow through on these areas that He has shown you. Ask God to help you reflect His love in your marriage. *Nothing* is too difficult for Him!

Note: If you will *not* be meeting with a discussion group or with another person to go through the Discussion Guide, please turn now to page 121 and go through the questions and new material for Week Two as if it were another daily lesson. You won't want to miss the additional insights found there!

Personal Study
Week Three

Experiencing the
Transformation of Christ

Lesson 1
"Our Relationship with God"

Reading: chapter 7

Spending Time with God

What gives us the open door to communicate with God? How can we truly come into His presence? Only through Christ's love and forgiveness. *"For You, Lord, are good, and ready to forgive, and abundant in lovingkindness to all who call upon You"* (Psalm 86:5). *"I will sing of the lovingkindness of the Lord forever; to all generations I will make known Your faithfulness with my mouth"* (Psalm 89:1). Meditate on these psalms and write down your thoughts about God's love for you.

Evaluating My Views

We have read about how far God's love reaches to restore us. And as we look at His love, we also confront our own corrupt sinful nature. The root of our sin is always pride. We proudly believe that we don't really need God's help. I don't want to accept that *my* nature is absolutely corrupt. Maybe hers, but not mine. But God says that we *all* fall short of His glory—even those women who seem to be descendants of Pollyanna.

The good news is that we can receive God's transforming power and love into our lives, thereby crucifying pride and establishing a right relationship with Him and with others. Only then can we live out His principles for a fulfilling life and marriage. Honestly ask yourself the following questions:

What roots of pride do I find in my life?

How has pride contributed to problems in my marriage?

Finding God's Perspective

God wants to draw us back to Himself and give us a new heart. He gave us a story in the book of Hosea that illustrates His grace and love lavishly poured upon a wayward wife to draw her back. The wife totally rejected her husband, Hosea, and ran off with other men. Yet Hosea wanted her back and demonstrated unending kindness and forgiveness toward her. In the end, he even had to buy his wife back, which is exactly what Christ did for us!

1. Read Hosea 1:2,3; 2:5–8; 3:1,2. How does this story picture the kind of love God has for us? (Hosea represents God's actions. Adultery is a symbol of our sin against God.)

2. According to 2 Corinthians 5:17, what does God desire to do with your life?

3. Have you put your faith in Christ, receiving His payment for your sins? If you know a specific time, write out when this life-changing decision occurred.

4. What does God tell us in Hebrews 7:25 and 13:5 about how long our relationship with Him will last?

Checking My Heart

1. Whether you have just begun your journey of faith in Christ or you have been a child of His for many years, God's desire is to transform your life to make you more and more like Christ. First John 1:9 says: *"If we confess our sins, He is faithful and righteous to forgive us our sins and to cleanse us from all unrighteousness."*

   To continue growing more like Christ, take a moment now and confess all known sin to God, including all thoughts that displease the Lord— especially any areas of pride.

2. First John 5:11–13 assures us of our position in God's Kingdom. Write down the promises you find in these verses for your own life.

3. Write out a short prayer of thanks to God for His incredible love and forgiveness toward you.

Allowing God to Transform Me

First John 5:11–13 is a critical verse for our foundation in Christ. When difficult times come, we can begin to doubt God's presence in our life. Therefore, repeat this verse frequently each day. It will help you walk steadily with God regardless of your circumstances.

Lesson 2
"Practicing Transparent Repentance"

Reading: chapter 8.

Spending Time with God

When you received Christ as your Savior, you also received His complete forgiveness. But if you still have unconfessed sin in your life, you will feel cut off from His peace and presence. And as long as you refuse to confess your sin, your actions will not reflect Christ's life within you, nor will you experience His power to change. That's an incredibly miserable state for a believer!

Can you recall a time when you felt this way? Psalm 32:3,4 reveals how David felt about his sin. *"When I kept silent about my sin, my body wasted away through my groaning all day long. For day and night Your hand was heavy upon me; my vitality was drained away as with the fever heat of summer."* Express to God your feelings about what sin has caused in your life.

Evaluating My Views

1. What is your perspective about Satan's goals for your life?

2. In what ways do you "toy" with sin and temptations?

3. Take the following "spiritual angiogram." Answer these questions about your heart attitude:

1. Is my heart broken and tender before the Lord?
2. Am I ready to be used for God's purposes at a moment's notice?
3. Is there any sin in my life that I have not yet confessed to God?
4. Am I practicing transparent repentance as soon as the Holy Spirit convicts me of sin?

Finding God's Perspective

1. Read John 10:10. Describe the long-term effects on your life of giving in to the enemy's temptations. Then describe the effects of following Christ.

2. God compares His work of removing sin and impurities from our lives with the purifying process of refining silver. According to Proverbs 25:4, what is the result of cleansing our lives of sin?

3. What attitude does God want us to have about this refining process (Hebrews 12:9–11)?

4. Using 1 John 1:9 and Ephesians 5:18 as a guide, describe the two steps in spiritual breathing.

Checking My Heart

One "little" sin can cost us everything! In 1 Samuel 10:1,8 and 13:7–14, we see an example in the life of King Saul. He didn't wait to offer sacrifices according to God's specific instructions—and it cost him his crown.

1. What excuses have you given for your actions when you disobeyed God's Word?

2. John the Baptist said, *"Therefore bring forth fruit in keeping with repentance"* (Matthew 3:8). What "fruits of repentance" need to happen in your own life now?

3. What acts of transparent repentance will you do to bring that about?

Allowing God to Transform Me

We need to remember what sin will cause in our life. Over the next week, look up the verses below and reflect on the destruction sin causes and on the peace and joy that obedience brings. Practice transparent repentance the moment you sense God's conviction.

SIN[1]	
• Steals joy (Ps.51:12)	• Opens the door to other sins (Is.30:1)
• Removes confidence (1 Jn.3:19–21)	• Causes frustration (Job 5:2)
• Brings guilt (Ps.51:3)	• Breaks fellowship (Is.59:1,2)
• Hinders usefulness for the Lord (1 Cor.3:1-3)	• Produces fear (Ps.34:4)
• Gives Satan the upper hand (2 Cor.2:9–11)	• Feeds the flesh (Rom.6)
• Quenches God's Spirit (1 Thes.5:18,19)	• Clouds eternal value system (Col.3:1,2)
• Brings physical damage (Ps.38:1–11; 31:10)	• Affects others (Gal.5:9)
• Causes ache in my bones (Ps.32:3,4)	• Brings disgrace on the name of the Lord (Rom.2:24)
• Destroys boldness (Prov.28:1)	• Makes me its slave (Jn.8:34, Gal.4:9)
• Breaks God's heart (Ps.78:41)	• *"Whatever is not from faith is sin"* (Rom.14:23)

Lesson 3
"Clear Conscience;
Conviction vs. Condemnation"

Reading: In chapter 8, review the sections titled "Restoring Relationships with Others" and "Conviction vs. Condemnation."

Spending Time with God

An impure heart cuts us off from experiencing God's presence. But through transparent repentance, we are made to be clean vessels again, usable for His perfect purposes. Psalm 51:10 says, *"Create in me a clean heart, O God, and renew a steadfast spirit within me."* Ask the Lord to continue purifying your life and to make you open to areas He may desire to uncover. Thank Him that everything He does in your life is done out of love.

Evaluating My Views

1. How do you think it would feel to have made things right with everyone in your life as much as you are able?

2. What are some failures in your past that seem to hinder your spiritual growth now?

3. Why do you think condemnation is such an effective tool of the enemy's?

Finding God's Perspective

1. Read Matthew 5:24 and Romans 12:18. What is God's attitude toward our relationship with others?

2. According to Hebrews 10:14, what is our standing as believers before God?

3. Describe what God wants our attitude to be as we maintain transparent repentance and a clear conscience (Hebrews 10:22,23).

Checking My Heart

"Having a clear conscience means that there is no one alive that I have ever wronged, offended, or hurt in any way that I have not gone back to and sought to make it right with both God and the individual."[2]

1. To have unhindered fellowship with God by establishing a clear conscience, of whom do you need to seek forgiveness? (Start with the hardest ones first.)

2. Do you understand the difference between God's conviction and Satan's condemnation? Are there areas in your life where Satan is defeating you through his relentless condemnation? In each space within the "Condemnation" side of the chart, describe a situation in which you are battling Satan's condemnation. Then fill in the side under "Conviction" as to how *God* wants you to deal with this particular issue.

Conviction	Condemnation
What is God's conviction concerning this issue?	What condemnation am I battling that comes from Satan?
How does God's conviction focus on a *specific* attitude or action regarding the issue I named? (Ex: "My impatience with my child was sin before God.")	How does Satan's condemnation focus *generally* on my character/who I am? (Ex: "I'm such a failure. I'm a terrible mother.")
What will happen when I confess this particular sin to God? (What changes will I see?)	What will likely happen in my particular situation if I continue listening to the enemy's condemnation? (Ex: further guilt, depression, defeat, poor self image.)
Action: When convicted, confess the specific sin to God (and others, if applicable), then claim His forgiveness. (1 John 1:9)	Action: When condemned, make sure you have confessed the specific sin to God (and others, if applicable), then claim the forgiveness of your sins and the righteousness of who you are in Christ. (Hebrews 10:14)

Allowing God to Transform Me

Oh, the blessed freedom that comes from knowing Christ, living in transparent repentance, and maintaining a clear conscience! Living in the freedom and forgiveness of Christ transforms our entire perspective on life, allowing us to demonstrate Christ's love to our husband, to our children, and to others. Praise God that *"He who began a good work in you will be faithful to complete it"* (Philippians 1:6).

Continue to practice transparent repentance by doing whatever is necessary to gain a clear conscience. Refuse Satan's condemnations and claim Hebrews 10:14.

Lesson 4
"I Don't Have to Choose Sin Anymore"

Reading: chapter 9

Spending Time with God

Consider how sin can become like a prison in a Christian's life. When you sin, you are taken captive by your lusts, selfishness, and pride. You are no longer free to live the victorious life in Christ that you want to live. And each time you sin, you are driven deeper into your prison. But God has flung open the prison doors! He has given us the power to live free of sin and to experience the peace of His forgiveness. Take a few moments to write a prayer of thanksgiving to God for the freedom we can experience through Christ.

Evaluating My Views

As you answer each of the following questions, develop a "before and after" picture of your spiritual journey. Examine your life before you were a Christian and after you took that step of faith in Christ. How has your life changed? (If you became a Christian as a child, compare your ideas as an immature Christian with your ideas as a more mature believer.)

1. What was different in your nature before your decision and after?
   Before:

   After:

2. Which sins were unbreakable habits before and what freedoms have you experienced after?

Before:

After:

3. What does the phrase, "As a Christian, I don't have to choose to sin anymore!" mean to you personally?

Finding God's Perspective

1. How does God say we should regard our sin (Colossians 3:3–10; Romans 6:6)?

2. According to 1 Corinthians 10:13, what temptations could prove too powerful to resist?

Dr. Bill Bright says, "Because of Christ's sacrifice, we are as dead to sin as a corpse is dead to this world. It cannot respond to any pleasure the world offers. No appealing aroma, glitzy picture or sultry music can cause that dead body to get up and indulge. In the same way, we are to consider ourselves dead to the desires and attractions of sin."[3]

3. How can you practice being dead to sin (Galatians 5:16; Colossians 3:5)?

Checking My Heart

In *The Wycliffe Bible Commentary*, we read: "Flesh and Spirit are opposites, locked in continual combat. If the Christian is walking by the power of one, he cannot be in the control of the other."[4]

1. How do you tend to handle temptations?

2. Describe the process of how you can now victoriously respond to any and every temptation that you encounter. (Look at Chapter 9, the section titled "Living Inside Out.")

Allowing God to Transform Me

Our lives are like a ball on a hill. The ball is either being pushed up the road or is rolling back down, but it cannot sit stationary on a hill. Similarly, the road climbing toward God is challenging and difficult, while the road descending away from Him is easy and comfortable.

Obedience and the resulting holiness in our everyday life doesn't just happen accidentally. They require purposeful choices. If we're not pushing up the hill toward godliness by intentional planning, then we'll immediately roll back down toward spiritual dullness by becoming hardened and insensitive to the Lord. Without a constant yielding of our lives to the Spirit, our old fleshly habit patterns will gravitate toward sin every time.

This very day, you are establishing a pattern of either trust and dependence on the Lord to flee from temptation or a pattern of depending on your own flesh and giving into temptation at every turn. The decisions you make today do affect your future. *"Do not be deceived: God cannot be mocked. A man reaps what he sows. The one who sows to please his sinful nature, from that nature will reap destruction; the one who sows to please the Spirit, from the Spirit will reap eternal life. Let us not become weary in doing good, for at the proper time we will reap a harvest if we do not give up"* (Galatians 6:7–9, NIV).

Ask God to remind you moment by moment to call on the strength of His Spirit within you; then choose to respond in righteousness.

Lesson 5
"On the Altar"

Reading: In chapter 9, review the section titled "On The Altar" to the end of the chapter.

Spending Time with God

Living "inside out" describes the Spirit-controlled life, which is choosing the Spirit over the flesh moment by moment. An essential part of Spirit-controlled living is to focus on God through praise. Read Psalm 89:11–16. Using the thoughts in this passage, tell God how wonderful and wise He is.

Evaluating My Views

1. Are you practicing living from the inside out, calling on the power of the Spirit and choosing righteousness? What changes have you noticed in your life as a result?

2. What are some areas of your life that have yet to be yielded to the Lord's full control (thoughts, attitudes, responses, actions)?

3. What keeps you from consistently yielding these areas to the Lord?

4. Why do you think dying to self is so hard?

Finding God's Perspective

The opposite of pride is humility. Humility is seeing myself through the eyes of the Lord. Humility is realizing how self-centered I am and how desperately I need God and His work in my life. The insightful Christian writer C.S.

Lewis said, "If anyone would like to acquire humility, I can, I think, tell him the first step. The first step is to realize that one is proud. And a biggish step, too. At least, nothing whatever can be done before it. If you think you are not conceited, it means you are very conceited indeed."[5]

1. What is God's attitude toward pride and humility (James 4:6)?

2. Read John 15:4,5. What does Jesus tell us is the result of trying to live in our own strength?

3. Recognizing our pride and our desperate need for Christ's work within us, how can we surrender to the Lord each day (Romans 6:13; 12:1)?

4. What does Psalm 145:9,17 tell us about being able to trust the Lord's will for our life?

Checking My Heart

I (Judy) often picture myself as a lump of clay on the altar, willing to be molded and shaped and used for whatever the Lord chooses (Isaiah 64:8). At first, it was frightening to be so vulnerable. But God's love toward us is so great! He promises that nothing can ever separate us from His love (Romans 8:38,39), and He gives us only that which is for our good (Romans 8:28). He made us, so He alone knows what is the very best for each of us. Therefore, *our* job is to stay on the altar, a living sacrifice for the Lord to work through. *God's* job is to transform us.

1. What do you need to do when you find yourself in control again and have crawled (or leaped) off His altar? (Refer to "On The Altar," chapter 9.)

2. Although we are emotional creatures, God's Word is always truer than anything we may feel. How do your daily choices illustrate this truth?

Allowing God to Transform Me

Paul wrote in Galatians 2:20, *"I have been crucified with Christ; and it is no longer I who live, but Christ lives in me; and the life which I now live in the flesh I live by faith in the Son of God, who loved me and gave Himself up for me."*

The Spirit-controlled life is a process that requires the moment-by-moment practice of yielding our life to the Lord and choosing His power to respond rightly. As we practice crucifying our prideful, selfish flesh by laying our life on His altar each day, we *will* see growth and change. God is committed to making us more and more like Christ.

Daily yielding your life, however, does not mean that everything will suddenly be perfect. Your spiritual growth in some areas may be slow and difficult. And if you have experienced a breakdown in your marital relationship because of your sinful choices or neglect, the rebuilding process may be difficult. *But don't get discouraged!* God is faithful! As you begin to practice dying on the altar daily, you *will* witness His transforming work in your life.

Start now by picturing yourself on an altar before the Lord. Make a commitment that you will give Him all that you are, and all that you will be—rich or poor, sick or well, dead or alive. As you practice this each day, you will be *amazed* at the effect on your entire life, your marriage, your children, and your relationships with all who love you!

Note: If you will *not* be meeting with a discussion group or with another person to go through the Discussion Guide, please turn now to page 124 and go through the questions and new material for Week Three as if it were another daily lesson. You won't want to miss the additional insights found there!

Depending on Christ and His Word

Lesson 1
"Our Desperate Need"

Reading: chapter 10

Spending Time with God

What we believe about God determines our entire worldview. That, in turn, affects everything we think and do. Bible teacher and writer Warren Wiersbe says, "When your theology is wrong, everything else follows."[1] Therefore, seeking to know God and His ways is worth far more than any other endeavor. He tells us to *"seek first His kingdom and His righteousness"* (Matthew 6:33).

As you read Jeremiah 9:23,24, ask God to give you an understanding of your desperate need to know Him: *"Thus says the Lord, 'Let not a wise man boast of his wisdom, and let not the mighty man boast of his might, let not a rich man boast of his riches; but let him who boasts boast of this, that he understands and knows Me, that I am the Lord who exercises lovingkindness, justice and righteousness on earth; for I delight in these things,' declares the Lord."*

Evaluating My Views

Our new lifestyle "in Christ" is completely different from our old life in our natural flesh (Galatians 5:17). Therefore, we constantly need to know God's perspective on every part of life. Compare what you thought about each of the following topics before you started this study with what God's Word says and your views now.

Subject	My Former Ideas	God's Word	My New Views
The consequences of adultery		Proverbs 6:32	
Having lustful thoughts toward another man		Matthew 5:27,28	
Pride		Proverbs 29:23	
My "human nature" apart from Christ		Psalm 16:2	

Finding God's Perspective

Paul reminds us that our old fleshly nature is completely corrupt when he says, *"For I know that nothing good dwells in me, that is, in my flesh"* (Romans 7:18).

1. According to Romans 12:1,2, what should our response be to this dilemma?

2. Why do we need to spend so much time with God (Isaiah 55:8,9)?

3. What is the result of not spending time with God and therefore cutting off the flow of Christ's power and transforming work (John 15:4,5)?

Checking My Heart

God tells us that *"as in water face reflects face, so the heart of man reflects man"* (Proverbs 27:19). Just like we see the reflection of our face in the water, so our heart reflects what we really are inside. A changed heart = changed actions. Take this "heart check" by honestly answering "yes" or "no" to each question.

Circle your answers:

1. Do I believe in my heart that apart from Christ's life in me, I am totally fallen and *"have no good thing"* (Psalm 16:2)?

                    YES   NO

2. Do I believe in my heart that without Christ working through me, I am capable of any sin, and I can do nothing that is truly good or of eternal value (John 15:4,5)?

                    YES   NO

Reflect on your answers. Were there any "no" answers? Were there any less-than-confident "yes" answers? When we come to truly see our fallen nature, we will confront our desperate need to be transformed by the Lord each day.

Allowing God to Transform Me

Begin every prayer time this week with Psalm 16:2 and John 15:5: *"I said to the Lord, 'You are my Lord; apart from you I have no good thing'"* (NIV). *"He who abides in Me, and I in him, he bears much fruit; for apart from Me you can do nothing."* Ask the Lord to inscribe these truths onto your heart and to show you your desperate need for His presence and His work in your life each day.

Also ask Him to show you what you are like apart from His transforming work. You will be appalled at what spews forth from your life! It will bring you to a very real understanding of your desperate need for His work in your life *every day.*

Lesson 2
"Daily Dependence on God Transforms Our Lives"

Reading: review chapter 10.

Spending Time with God

As we grow in knowing God, it is critically important that we develop a *biblical* view of who He is. We do this by studying His Word. It is also vitally important to be involved in a Bible-believing local church that helps guide us into a correct, biblical knowledge of God. As you read 1 Chronicles 29:10–13, ask God to help you grow in understanding His ways.

"So David blessed the Lord in the sight of all the assembly; and David said, 'Blessed are You, O Lord God of Israel our father, forever and ever. Yours, O Lord, is the greatness and the power and the glory and the victory and the majesty, indeed everything that is in the heavens and the earth; Yours is the dominion, O Lord, and You exalt Yourself as head over all. Both riches and honor come from You, and You rule over all, and in Your hand is power and might; and it lies in Your hand to make great and to strengthen everyone. Now therefore, our God, we thank You, and praise Your glorious name.'"

Evaluating My Views

Is your Christian walk consistent or inconsistent? Are you depending on God or on your own efforts? Think about the following areas of your relationship with your husband and with others. Which of these areas are most difficult for you in demonstrating a consistent spiritual life? Mark one or more.

- ❑ Temper outbursts/ patience
- ❑ Lust/ pure thoughts
- ❑ Selfishness/ selflessness
- ❑ Sharp tongue/ words of edification
- ❑ Holding grudges/ forgiving
- ❑ Self-dependent/ relying on God

- ❑ Irritable spirit/ Spirit-controlled
- ❑ Critical spirit/ accepting
- ❑ Proud/ humble
- ❑ **Want to be served/ demonstrating servanthood**
- ❑ Deceit/ honesty

Finding God's Perspective

Because of our fallen flesh, we can never be spiritually consistent on our own. That's why we must yield our lives to the Lord each day, depending on His transforming work through us. Only then can we be available and ready for God to use at a moment's notice. For example, in the Old Testament book of Esther, a regular Jewish girl finds herself catapulted into the role of queen. More than that, she then faces a life-or-death decision of whether to step forward and reveal her Jewish nationality to try and save her people, or to remain quiet. Esther *did* step forward, and in so doing, saved the Jews from slaughter. That was her moment.

1. What did Esther's uncle, Mordecai, say to her in Esther 4:14?

2. What does God tell us can happen if we don't keep our heart tender to the Lord each day (Hebrews 3:12,13)?

3. What happens in our lives as we die daily and allow Christ's Spirit to transform us (Galatians 5:22,23)?

We never know when God may choose to use us. And if we are out of fellowship with Him, we may miss an incredible opportunity. It won't change God's plans. He will always accomplish His will regardless—but I don't want to miss out on being His special instrument!

Checking My Heart

Apart from Christ, we can do nothing of eternal value. With Christ living through us, we can do all He asks of us. If we remain dependent on the Lord, He can use us at a moment's notice. Yet we are so weak!

1. How does God tell us to view our weaknesses in 2 Corinthians 12:9,10?

God will *"equip you in every good thing to do His will, working in us that which is pleasing in His sight, through Jesus Christ"* (Hebrews 13:21) if you will just lay your life on His altar and let Him work!

We've looked at pride and humility. Pride says, "I can do pretty well today without yielding myself in absolute dependence on Christ's help." Humility realizes my weaknesses and that I have no means within myself with which to bring forth any righteousness, any goodness, any kindness. Without time in His presence, my perspective will be skewed, my words will be fleshly, and my attitude will be selfish.

2. What is my perspective each morning on how I will get through the day?

3. What do my daily choices reveal about my dependence on the Lord?

4. What differences can people recognize in my life that point to consistent time spent with the Creator?

Allowing God to Transform Me

Continue to ask God to implant in your heart the conviction that apart from Christ's Spirit, you have "no good thing," and that apart from Christ's work through you, you can do nothing of eternal value. Continue praying Psalm 16:2 and John 15:5, and review the verses in the box toward the end of Chapter 10 until this truth drives you to desperate, daily dependence on the Lord.

Lesson 3
"The Effect of God's Word in Our Lives"

Reading: chapter 11

Spending Time with God

Psalm 119 emphasizes the importance of God's Word. Write down your thoughts under each verse about why it is so important for us to know His Word:

119:98–100 —"Your commandments make me wiser than my enemies, for they are ever mine. I have more insight than all my teachers, for Your testimonies are my meditation. I understand more than the aged, because I have observed Your precepts."

119:105 – "Your word is a lamp to my feet and a light to my path."

119:165 – "Those who love Your law have great peace, and nothing causes them to stumble."

Listening to God as He speaks to us through the Bible allows us to know Him and to grow more like Christ. Thank the Lord for giving us His precious Word.

Evaluating My Views

Many Christians believe the Bible and believe that it is important, yet they don't make the effort to know it well. Take this little quiz about the Bible. See how familiar you are with God's Book.

1. How many books does the Bible contain?
2. Which book in the Bible has the creation account?
3. Which book tells the history of the early church?
4. Name the person who wrote the greatest number of books in the New Testament.

How did you do? (Check your answers with those at the end of this lesson.) However, far more important than knowing *about* the Bible is knowing the *author* of the Bible—God. That is our goal for digging into God's Word.

Finding God's Perspective

1. What does God tell us about being able to trust His Word even when life's circumstances seem contradictory (Psalm 119:160; Proverbs 19:21)?

2. What should our response be to God's Word (1 Thessalonians 2:13)?

3. In Psalm 19:7–11, we see changes that the Word can produce in our lives. What are some of them?

Checking My Heart

1. What kinds of situations make me doubt or question God's Word?

2. What thoughts do I frequently nurture that are not in line with God's truth?

3. What choices and actions do I find myself making that are not based on God's Word?

Allowing God to Transform Me

What kinds of answers did you give for "Checking My Heart"? Can you say with the psalmist, *"I esteem right all Your precepts concerning everything, I hate every false way"* (Psalm 119:128)? Allow God to change these areas so that they conform to His Word. Pray about each area now, asking God to transform your heart through the power of the Holy Spirit. Search God's Word for His wisdom on difficult-to-understand areas. If needed, practice transparent repentance.

(Answers to questions: 1. 66, 2. Genesis, 3. Acts, 4. The Apostle Paul)

Lesson 4
"Establishing Daily Time with God"

Reading: Review chapter 11 from the section titled "What To Study" to the end of the chapter.

Spending Time with God

Ask God to give you a deep desire to study, read, and apply His Word to your life. *"As the deer pants for the water brooks, so my soul pants for You, O God"* (Psalm 42:1).

Evaluating My Views

We are going to discuss how to study God's Word. To prepare yourself, write your answers to these questions:

• What are you curious about or interested to learn about in God's Word?

• Is there a topic of which you would like to know God's perspective? What is it?

• Which Bible character fascinates you?

• What attributes or aspects of God's character seem unclear to you?

Finding God's Perspective

1. According to Hebrews 4:12, what does the Bible do in our lives?

Andrew Murray writes: "There may be a study and knowledge of the Word, in which there is but little real fellowship with the living God. But there is also a reading of the Word, in the very presence of the Father, and under the leading of the Spirit, in which the Word comes to us in living power from God Himself; it is to us the very voice of the Father, a real personal blessing and strength, and awakens the response of a living faith that reaches the heart of God again."[2]

2. What does this quote say about our Quiet Times with God?

3. What should we do to enter into the presence of the living God (Matthew 6:6; Psalm 131:2)?

Checking My Heart

One thing is absolutely 100 percent guaranteed—time with the Lord won't "just happen." If you wait until you are motivated and it seems easy to spend time with Him, you'll find yourself one day standing before His throne without ever having gotten to know Him! Time in God's presence truly is the most important thing you will do each day. To help you start spending daily time with God, fill out this Quiet Time chart:

I am going to meet with God at _____ each day.
                                            place

The time I will spend with Him is from _____ to _____

I will study this topic/ issue/ book of the Bible: _____

To make this Quiet Time a reality, I need to: _____

Allowing God to Transform Me

Ask God to continue implanting in your heart the reason why it is so utterly critical for you to cling to Him each day in order to be renewed and transformed through His Word and His presence. As you spend time in His presence, begin recording what God impresses on your mind during your daily Quiet Time.

Lesson 5
"Dying, Adoring, Confessing, and Arming"

Reading: chapter 12.

Spending Time with God

Christ taught us to recognize and praise God for His virtues: *"Our Father who is in heaven, hallowed be Your name"* (Matthew 6:9). In His Name resides all that He is. Read these psalms and spend a few moments praising God right now for His holy name. He is worthy of all our praise!

> Psalm 148:13 - *"Let them praise the name of the Lord, for His name alone is exalted; His glory is above earth and heaven."*

> Psalm 99:3 - *"Let them praise Your great and awesome name; holy is He."*

Evaluating My Views

God tells us that when we cover ourselves with His armor each day, we will be able to stand firm in every battle (Ephesians 6:13). Describe how donning each piece of God's armor can affect your entire day. (Refer back to "The Armor of God" section in the book if needed.)

1. Girding your loins with truth:

2. Putting on the breastplate of righteousness:

3. Shodding your feet with the gospel of peace:

4. Taking up the shield of faith:

5. Putting on the helmet of salvation:

6. Taking up the sword of the Spirit:

Finding God's Perspective

Christ lived with more demands on Him and more people seeking His attention than we will ever experience. Everywhere He went, hundreds of people crowded Him just to touch His garment or to ask Him questions. *"But He Himself would often slip away to the wilderness and pray"* (Luke 5:16). If God on earth frequently needed a quiet, lonely place in which to pray, how much more do you and I!

But to be honest, almost every day I (Judy) face a battle when it comes to pray. As an active person, I struggle to sit still. However, that isn't the real battle. The *real* war is against my pride. Prayer humbles my soul to seek and depend on God, thus crucifying pride. And my pride doesn't *like* to be crucified!

1. Read Luke 18:9–14, and describe the prayer attitude God desires.

2. In Luke 6:12–16 we see Jesus' example of prayer just before an important time in His ministry. Read these verses and describe what Jesus did.

3. God loves for us to pray specifically. He provides many examples throughout Scripture of His specific answers to specific prayers. King David asked the Lord specific questions when he was being attacked by the Philistines. Read 2 Samuel 5:17–25. How can this be an example for your prayers?

4. How can unconfessed sin affect your prayer life (Psalm 66:18; Isaiah 59:1,2)?

Checking My Heart

Ask yourself these questions about your prayer life:

- Is pride and self-dependence keeping me from meeting humbly with God in prayer?

- Am I practicing daily (hourly) laying my life on the altar for God to do with as He chooses?

- Do I find adoration toward the Lord to be easy or difficult? Would knowing more about His attributes help me praise Him more fully?

- Is there any sin that has begun to fester and decay in my life? What keeps me from confessing that now?

Now ask yourself: Will I practice putting on each piece of God's armor this week to protect and prepare every part of my life against the devil's schemes?

Allowing God to Transform Me

The following Quiet Time model can be adapted for your own use. As you have your Quiet Time according to your schedule from the previous lesson, begin practicing the four steps of Dying, Adoring, Confessing, and Arming. Practice putting on each piece of God's armor, and keep His armor in mind throughout the day to remind you to flee from sin and to resist the enemy.

Note: If you will *not* be meeting with a discussion group or with another person to go through the Discussion Guide, please turn now to page 127 and go through the questions and new material for Week Four as if it were another daily lesson. You won't want to miss the additional insights found there!

Quiet Time Model

Go to your quiet place where you can focus on the Lord.

Open in prayer:

Ask God to meet with you, and ask Him to give you His insight into His Word. *"Open my eyes, that I may behold wonderful things from Your law"* (Psalm 119:18).

Time in the Bible:

As you do your Bible study, write down on a piece of paper everything that ministers, convicts, or speaks to your heart. (If you sense God's conviction, practice transparent repentance right then so that your fellowship with Him will remain unhindered.)

Time in Prayer:

Dying: Lay your life on the altar before God: "Rich or poor, sick or well, dead or alive, I am completely Yours, Lord, to do with whatever You choose."

Adoration: Praise Him for His marvelous attributes, such as His grace, His love, His faithfulness, His wisdom, His power, His majesty, etc.

Confession: Ask God to search your heart, praying Psalm 139:23,24: *"Search me, O God, and know my heart; try me and know my anxious thoughts; and see if there be any hurtful way in me, and lead me in the everlasting way."* Immediately confess anything He may show you.

Arming: Put on each piece of His armor *"so that you will be able to stand firm against the schemes of the devil"* (Ephesians 6:11):

Gird your loins with truth: Pray: "Lord, I gird my loins with Your truth. Please weave Your Word into my life as part of the fabric of my being." Then ask God to apply in your life the things that He showed you from your Bible study time. Pray through the things that you wrote down. Also review any verse you are committing to memory at this time.

Put on the breastplate of righteousness: Pray: "Lord Jesus, I put You on as my breastplate of righteousness because I have no good besides You, and I can do nothing of eternal value apart from You" (Psalm 16:2,

John 15:5). Picture "putting on" Christ, and ask Him to speak with your lips, think with your mind, and see through your eyes that entire day, in every circumstance.

Shod your feet with the gospel of peace: Pray: "Lord, I shod my feet with the preparation of the gospel of peace in order to flee from evil and to run to You for Your strength and protection." Picture fleeing from any situation that you know is not honoring to the Lord.

Take up the shield of faith: Pray: "Lord, I take up the shield of faith." Then pray "by faith" for the prayer requests on your heart, demonstrating your complete dependence on His answers. Trust that His will is perfect and good, carried out in complete love.

Take the helmet of salvation: Pray: "Lord, I put on the helmet of salvation." Then picture His helmet covering your eyes, ears, and mind to keep you from seeing, hearing, or thinking anything that displeases Him.

Take up the sword of the Spirit: Pray: "Lord, I take up the sword of the Spirit and ask that You will remind me to resist Satan according to Your Word throughout this day." Then when a temptation or condemnation comes along, say aloud, "Satan, I resist you in the name of the Lord Jesus Christ" according to James 4:7.

End your prayer time by thanking God for the work He is doing in your life and in those around you—especially your husband and your family. Then rise up *"in the strength of His might"* (Ephesians 6:10)!

Lesson 1
"Elements of Obedience"

Reading: chapter 13.

Spending Time with God

God tells us that when Christ's Spirit lives within us, we not only have the power to obey, but we also have the desire to obey: *"For it is God who works in you to will and to act according to his good purpose"* (Philippians 2:13, NIV, emphasis added). Thank the Lord that He gives us the desire and the ability to walk in righteousness. What a gift He has given us!

Evaluating My Views

Look at the contrast between obedience and disobedience found in these verses:

Obedience: *"I considered my ways and turned my feet to Your testimonies. I hastened and did not delay to keep Your commandments"* (Psalm 119:59,60).

Disobedience: *"Why do you call Me, 'Lord, Lord,' and do not do what I say?"* (Luke 6:46).

Which one do you think best describes your daily choices? List some specific choices that illustrate this.

Finding God's Perspective

The Bible shows us many examples of the results of obedience and disobedience. Contrast Joshua and Saul, two leaders of ancient Israel. How are they different in their approaches to obedience? Write your answers in the chart:

	Joshua	Saul
The beginning of his ministry for God	Numbers 27:15–23	1 Samuel 9:1,2; 10:1,9,10
His actions	Joshua 11:15	1 Samuel 15:10,11
His final days	Joshua 23:1–3; 24:29–31	1 Samuel 28:5,6,17–19; 31:2–6

Checking My Heart

Obedience is our responsibility—the outcome is *God's* responsibility. God measures our success or failure 100 percent by our obedience to Him. When God directs us to do something, we are to obey regardless of the results. The world, and even many Christians, may not always understand. But as the apostles said, *"We must obey God rather than men"* (Acts 5:29). God deems those a success who totally obey *His* voice.

Fill in the three elements of obedience mentioned in chapter 13:

1. Obedience is a _____, never based on my feelings.
2. Obedience is _____, because delay leads me into ever-increasing sin.
3. Obedience is _____, following God's *entire* Word.

Which of these three seems the hardest for you? Why?

We always marvel at how some pastor or dynamic spiritual leader can end up in adultery. But "big" sins always start with one "little" choice of hardening our heart toward something the Lord has said. And that little choice makes the next choice of disobedience twice as easy. From there, it's a greased slide down the slope. And we are *all* one choice away from beginning that slide. What do you need to do to stay off that slide?

Allowing God to Transform Me

Obedience to God's Word always leads me into righteousness. Each morning as I gird my loins with God's truth, I'm really saying, *"I choose to live by 'every word that proceeds out of the mouth of God'"* (Matthew 4:4). He says to flee sexual temptation, so I choose to avoid all enticing situations. He says to love the person who treats me poorly, so I choose to demonstrate His love regardless of feelings.

But walking in obedience requires a conscious effort. Write down three difficult areas in which you will obey God and His Word by the power of His Spirit this week. Remember to call on His power to obey moment by moment.

Lesson 2
"Motivations Behind Our Obedience"

Reading: Review chapter 13 from "Motivations for Obedience" to the end.

Spending Time with God

The Bible tells us that *"we love, because He first loved us"* (1 John 4:19). Christ says that our obedience demonstrates our love for the Lord. *"He who has My commandments and keeps them is the one who loves Me"* (John 14:21). Our love for God motivates us to obey Him. Meditate on this thought, then write a short love letter to God.

Evaluating My Views

If we fail to comprehend God's love and the enormity of Christ's sacrifice for us, then in turn we will lack love for Him. When that happens, we can fall into legalism. Legalism attempts to earn God's love by performing. But we don't need to "earn" His love—we already have it in fullest measure! However, it's easy for us to edge away from love into legalism. What may begin as a labor of love for God can turn into a set of rules. Rate yourself in the following areas of service to God. Draw a mark on the line where you think you are in the continuum. Then as you go through the lesson, keep these legalistic areas in mind so that you can surrender them once again to the Lord for *His* work through you.

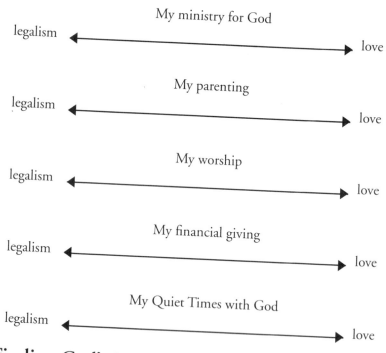

My ministry for God

legalism ←————————————————→ love

My parenting

legalism ←————————————————→ love

My worship

legalism ←————————————————→ love

My financial giving

legalism ←————————————————→ love

My Quiet Times with God

legalism ←————————————————→ love

Finding God's Perspective

When we find ourselves trying to earn God's love or favor, we need to repent of self-righteous efforts that count for nothing (John 15:5) and yield our life back to the One who works His righteousness through us. Legalism and disobedience both are corrected by having proper motivations for obeying and serving God.

1. What does Psalm 25:10 say about obedience motivated by trust?

2. Proverbs 1:32,33 gives us a contrast between disobedience and obedience. How do these verses encourage us to obey for our own protection?

3. What can we learn from Abraham and Moses about being motivated to obey because of our future rewards (Hebrews 11:8–10,24–26)?

4. Contrast the situations that brought Paul joy and sorrow in Philemon 7 and 2 Timothy 4:14. What does this tell us about our obedience or disobedience and its effects on others?

Checking My Heart

Let's take another "spiritual angiogram" concerning obedience:

- Have you predetermined to obey whatever God shows you each day?
- Do you see in your life a pattern of responding to God's conviction with immediate obedience, or do you tend to delay, demonstrating *dis*obedience?
- Have you determined to obey *all* of God's Word, even if it seems hard, inconvenient, or downright painful to do so?
- Do you find motivation to obey the Lord because you trust Him and understand that obedience protects you from consequences you can't possibly see?
- Do you find it motivating to obey because God promises blessings and rewards to those who keep His statutes?
- Do you believe that *no act of disobedience is insignificant?* Consequently, do you understand how hardness in your heart affects your choices and your actions, thereby affecting everyone around you?

Allowing God to Transform Me

We've spent a good deal of time talking about living the Spirit-controlled life and having daily time with the Lord. Why? Because these are *the two most essential elements* in any faithful believer's life. One without the other leads to sin, whether that is infidelity or any other act of disobedience. Ask God to continue developing in you an understanding of your desperate need for His Word and His work in and through you each day. As you "put on Christ" each day, ask Him to remind you to obey instantly and completely, drawing on His power to do so. You will be amazed at the results!

Lesson 3
"Confronting Integrity"

Reading: chapter 14.

Spending Time with God

Whatever we focus on determines what we will become. If our eyes remain on the Lord, He fills our mind with His truth and we become more and more like Christ. But if we fill our minds with romantic soap operas, sensual music, and trash from the Internet, our minds become like a garbage landfill.

As believers, we are actually God's temple! Therefore, God's Word calls us to holiness. Read and ponder 2 Corinthians 6:16–7:1. Make greater purity and integrity a focus for this study.

Evaluating My Views

Just as Christ chastised the Pharisees for washing the outside of the cup while leaving it full of filth on the inside (Luke 11:39), we need to deliberately scrutinize all that we do, both privately and publicly, examining each choice to make sure it lines up with God's Word.

List the influences and choices in your life that are poor examples of integrity. These may be influences such as certain types of movies, books, magazines, and music that encourage impure thoughts or unbiblical behavior. Or you may write down activities such as work-related interactions that draw you toward another man. Perhaps you may list a friend who influences you to make wrong choices.

Finding God's Perspective

God convicted a policeman about a lie he told during work. Though he knew the consequences could be severe, he decided it was more important to have a clear conscience before the Lord and to restore his integrity than to cover the lie. So he revealed the truth to his boss—and lost his job. Did he regret that decision? He said later that restoring a clear conscience and regaining his integrity had given him such freedom and peace that he knew he had made the right decision. Even if maintaining integrity means losing the riches of this world, we must choose to live for the eternal.

1. According to 1 Peter 1:14–16, what should our standard be?

2. What does 1 John 2:15,16 tell us about loving the things of this world?

The Lord rewards integrity with gifts that last eternally and exceed *anything* we could have gained in this life. So although integrity may be costly for the moment, it is worth everything.

3. What kind of perspective on life and integrity does Psalm 103:15–18 give?

4. Living a life of integrity really begins where (Matthew 16:24)?

Checking My Heart

1. Jesus says in Luke 16:10, *"He who is faithful in a very little thing is faithful also in much; and he who is unrighteous in a very little thing is unrighteous also in much."* Describe what this passage reveals about your life and what you need to change.

2. Think of a situation you face right now that is testing your integrity. What are the choices you have?

3. How can you maintain your integrity even if it costs you something?

Allowing God to Transform Me

Follow through with your choices of integrity in the questions above. First, ask God to help you choose wisely. Then determine ways you can maintain your integrity. Also use your list under "Evaluating My Views" to help remind you of places where you need to be vigilant with your integrity, starting now.

Lesson 4
"Practicing Integrity"

Reading: Review chapter 14.

Spending Time with God

Living a life of integrity does not mean retreating into a cave and removing ourselves from the world's influence. Christ clearly tells us to be light *in* a darkened world. We must live among nonbelievers in such a way that our lives point them to Christ. On the other hand, we must keep ourselves from becoming entangled in the world's philosophies and sinful activities. Read the verses below and ask God to help you live in such a way that others see Christ in you.

"Let your light shine before men in such a way that they may see your good works, and glorify your Father who is in heaven" (Matthew 5:16).

"Dear friends, I urge you, as aliens and strangers in the world, to abstain from sinful desires, which war against your soul. Live such good lives among the pagans that, though they accuse you of doing wrong, they may see your good deeds and glorify God on the day he visits us" (1 Peter 2:11,12 NIV).

Evaluating My Views

Answer this integrity checklist, writing yes or no at the end of each question:

1. Does my behavior change when no one is looking or no one knows?

2. Do I swear under my breath?

3. Do I exaggerate or lie in "little" areas (like my weight)?

4. Do I think speeding to get my children to school on time is more important than modeling integrity before them?

5. Do I daydream about things God considers impure?

6. Do my shelves contain books, movies, magazines, CDs, or games that denigrate God's holy name?

7. Does my home contain "decorations" that are actually items of pagan worship?

How did you do? Did you answer any of these with a "yes"? Focus on these areas as you complete the day's study.

Finding God's Perspective

1. What instructions do you find in Psalm 51:6?

2. Which area of integrity does Proverbs 8:7,8 describe, and how can you apply this Scripture?

3. What does God specifically instruct you to do in Titus 2:11–14?

4. What is the contrast found in 1 John 2:3–6?

Checking My Heart

Prayerfully read Psalm 119:1–5:
"How blessed are those whose way is blameless, who walk in the law of the Lord.
How blessed are those who observe His testimonies, who seek Him with all their heart.
They also do no unrighteousness; they walk in His ways.
You have ordained Your precepts, that we should keep them diligently.
Oh that my ways may be established to keep Your statutes!"

Now go back and look at your "yes" answers in the "Evaluating My Views" section. Write down specific actions you need to take to bring these areas in line with God's standard of holiness and integrity.

Allowing God to Transform Me

Take several minutes of silence, allowing God to search your heart for any practices that you have accepted as normal, but which are really sin. Write down anything He brings to mind and what you need to do to re-establish integrity. Ask Him to help you follow through in making righteous choices.

Lesson 5
"Integrity and the Media"

Reading: chapter 15

Spending Time with God

"I will walk within my house in the integrity of my heart. I will set no worthless thing before my eyes; I hate the work of those who fall away; it shall not fasten its grip on me. A perverse heart shall depart from me; I will know no evil" (Psalm 101:2–4).

Which area of the media has the greatest allure for you? television? movies? books? magazines? the Internet? Select one and use it throughout this lesson to help you develop habits of integrity. If several areas present a challenge for you, work through this lesson again, focusing on each of the other media areas that trouble you. To begin, ask God to help you break any impure habits you may have regarding your selected area.

Evaluating My Views

Concerning the media area that poses the greatest purity challenge to you:

1. How much time do you spend on it each week?

2. What kinds of impure thoughts and actions are encouraged by participation in unholy aspects of this media?

3. By allowing impurity from this media into your life, how has this made you less sensitive to God's Spirit?

Finding God's Perspective

1. What action does 1 Thessalonians 5:21,22 tell us to take?

2. What always remains one of our strongest forms of defense against temptation (Psalm 119:11; Proverbs 7:1,3)?

3. What else does God tell us is critical for keeping our lives and actions pure and holy (Proverbs 11:14; 12:15)?

Checking My Heart

Read Psalm 101:2–4 again. Then answer these questions to find your I.Q. (Integrity Quotient):

- Can I honestly say that every part of Psalm 101:2–4 is true for me and my home?

- Do I justify attending movies or watching TV shows that contain content God calls perverted and impure?

- Do I tend to believe that implanting such images in my mind will not harm my life or my spiritual sensitivity?

- Am I willing to take the "R-rated Challenge?"

- Am I willing to begin examining *everything* I set before my eyes according to God's standards and to get rid of my cable or satellite service, or even the TV itself, if God directs me to do so?

- Have I given into temptations to view pornography? If not, have I pre-established guards and filters to keep me from falling into the quicksand of pornography? If so, am I willing to confess that to God and to my husband?

Allowing God to Transform Me

Go to God in prayer, asking Him to show you ways to re-establish integrity and purity in the area(s) which He has revealed. This can range from turning off your TV and setting up accountability in these areas, to canceling your cable subscription and your Internet access.

Then every day as you shod your feet with the gospel of peace (Ephesians 6:15), picture fleeing from evil by turning off your TV or your computer whenever anything unholy comes before your eyes. It's worth whatever it takes to have a pure heart before the Lord!

Note: If you will *not* be meeting with a discussion group or with another person to go through the Discussion Guide, please turn now to page 130 and go through the questions and new material for Week Five as if it were another daily lesson. You won't want to miss the additional insights found there!

Living Out Christ's Love and Caring for Your Marriage

Lesson 1
"Love and Feelings"

Reading: chapter 16

Spending Time with God

We have seen how living the Spirit-controlled life, spending daily time with the Lord, and living with integrity make a dramatic difference in our lives. But do they affect our marriage? Yes, in *every* way! When we remain in a right relationship with God, then His work within us *will* affect our marriage. But in order to be rightly related to our Lord, and consequently to our husband, we must also understand God's unique perspective on love.

Meditate on these verses that show the Lord's incredible love, and thank God that we can love Him and others because He first loved us:

> John 3:16 – *"For God so loved the world that He gave his one and only Son, that whoever believes in him shall not perish but have eternal life"* (NIV).

> Romans 5:8 – *"But God demonstrates His own love toward us, in that while we were yet sinners, Christ died for us."*

> 1 John 3:1 – *"See how great a love the Father has bestowed on us, that we would be called children of God; and such we are."*

Evaluating My Views

The weddings of past generations emphasized godly love and commitment to your mate. The vows to "love and honor" were taken more seriously. The ceremony held an air of solemn importance. Today, the average marriage ceremony focuses on romantic love, the vows are often flippant, and the ceremony may be as frivolous as skydiving or being married underwater. Often people will say, "Aren't they a cute couple? They're so in love."

While it's wonderful that the bride and groom gaze at one another with starry-eyed rapture, the important issue is what *kind* of love their nuptials are based upon. Is their marriage founded merely upon a romantic infatuation soon to wither and fade, or are they committed to one another based on the unconditional love of 1 Corinthians 13, demonstrated through patience, kindness, humility, selflessness, and forgiveness?

1. What kind of views do your friends have about marriage and the marriage ceremony?

2. How have your views on marriage changed since beginning this study?

3. How has this change affected your marriage?

Finding God's Perspective

1. Read 1 Corinthians 13. How does God's definition of love differ from the views you mentioned in the questions above?

2. Why is pursuing emotional love in an attraction outside your marriage as foolish as trying to build a house on a sand dune (Matthew 7:24–27)?

3. How did Jesus demonstrate selfless love (Philippians 2:5–8)?

4. We are told to *"have this attitude [of selfless love] in yourselves which was also in Christ Jesus"* (Philippians 2:5). What practical ways can you demonstrate the Philippians 2:5–8 type of love in your marriage?

To regard my husband as more important than myself means that I *choose* to focus on meeting his needs above my own, just as Christ chose to give His life to meet my needs. This is not saying that my husband is better than I am. Instead, I'm recognizing my high calling to serve him just as Christ served us. *"Let all that you do be done in love"* (1 Corinthians 16:14).

Checking My Heart

1. Apply the Philippians 2:3 "gold standard" to *"do nothing from selfishness or empty conceit, but with humility of mind regard one another as more important than yourselves"* specifically to a conflict in your marriage.

2. Describe how your feelings have worked against your marriage at times.

3. Which feelings do you need to put under the Spirit's control?

Allowing God to Transform Me

Write a "bullet prayer" that you can shoot up to God whenever your feelings get out of line in your marriage relationship. This week, pray that prayer each time your feelings begin to overshadow the need to demonstrate godly, sacrificial love.

Lesson 2
"Godly Love Protects Your Marriage"

Reading: In chapter 16, review the four points under the section "Love and Protection."

Spending Time with God

Dr. Bill Bright says of his marriage:

> Vonette and I have had 53 wonderful years of marriage, but had we not been spiritually minded, had we not both sought the will of the Lord, it would have been a disaster. Vonette is a very strong-willed woman and I, too, am very strong-willed. Each of us naturally has tended to want our own way and do our own thing. But from even during our engagement period before the wedding ceremony, we determined that with the help of the Holy Spirit we would seek first the kingdom of God and we would each invite our Lord Jesus to direct our lives and our marriage . . . He is the one who has preserved us through the years and will continue to do so as we walk in the Spirit and invite His control of our thoughts, attitudes, actions, motives, desire, and words.[1]

Matthew 6:33 tells us to *"seek first His kingdom and His righteousness, and all these things will be added to you."* If you haven't done so yet today, lay your life on His altar, seeking Him first. Then ask Jesus to direct every aspect of your life, including your marriage.

Evaluating My Views

Think of a recent incident in your marriage when your husband and you strongly disagreed. Evaluate how you approached the disagreement by writing out the ways you accomplished or failed to apply the following four points in the conflict:

1. I denied my own selfish desires.

2. I forgave or asked for forgiveness quickly.

3. I took any negative thoughts captive before and after the disagreement.

4. I gave up my rights for the sake of our relationship.

Finding God's Perspective

1. What does Proverbs 12:4 say about our roles as wives?

2. What principle can you apply to your closest friend (your husband) that Jesus gave us in John 15:13?

3. How does Ephesians 4:32 apply to your marriage?

Checking My Heart

Answer these questions about your family relationships, and write what changes you need to make:

• Do I depend on my feelings in order to demonstrate love?

• Do I allow my thoughts to dwell on all my husband's irritating quirks, or do I take those thoughts captive?

- Do I refuse to ask forgiveness, or do my children hear me apologize frequently, asking and giving forgiveness to my husband and to them?

- Do I hang onto my rights, becoming angry when my husband doesn't do things "my way," or do I practice yielding those rights to God?

- Does my family see me running to Christ for His strength because I understand that the quality of every single relationship in my life is dependent upon my relationship with Him?

Allowing God to Transform Me

If God has uncovered an area revealing a lack of His godly love, please stop and take the steps below that are necessary to make that area right.

★ Confess deep-seated pride and selfishness in your life and how that affects your marriage and family.

★ Ask forgiveness of someone.

★ Confess having dwelt on your husband's faults instead of thanking God for his qualities.

★ Yield to God the rights to which you are tenaciously clinging.

Whatever God has shown you, purpose to make these areas right immediately so that you can once again experience His forgiveness and peace and demonstrate His sacrificial love.

Lesson 3
"Our Testimony of Love"

Reading: Review in chapter 16 the sections titled "A Testimony to our Children" and "A Testimony to the World."

Spending Time with God

Consider the kind of love the Lord has for us: "*He who did not spare His own Son, but delivered Him over for us all, how will He not also with Him freely give us all things?*" (Romans 8:32). The horrific death Jesus faced was not something He was forced to do. He chose this death for our sakes. Thank Him for what He was willing to do out of love for you.

Evaluating My Views

How much of an influence are you on your world? Jesus came and died so that He and His followers would influence the world for God's glory. One way His love is demonstrated to the world is through the actions of believers. Evaluate your testimony to the world in these two areas:

1. When my children (or other close family members) look at how I treat my husband, what kind of influence have I been? (List both the good influences and the bad.)

2. When my neighbors or coworkers look at my marriage relationship, what do they see? (List the good and bad of what they see.)

Finding God's Perspective

We cannot control what our spouse does, and God does not expect us to. Our job is not to "fix" our husbands. But God *does* require that we display His love in all that we do. In turn, His love will influence our husbands, children, and many other people around us.

1. What kind of marriage relationship should you be building so that the world can see Jesus in you (Proverbs 31:10–12; 1 Peter 3:3,4)?

2. What does God expect us to produce in our lives (Galatians 5:22,23)?

3. How will this benefit your children?

Checking My Heart

Children imitate what they see demonstrated at home. It's so easy to let our behavior slide at home because that's where we feel most comfortable. Evaluate the following areas to see what you are modeling that your children will imitate:

My speech:

What I view or read:

Where I go during my free time:

My attitude and words to my husband:

How I handle minor crises:

How I spend money:

Allowing God to Transform Me

Which one of the areas above is your weakest? Continually practice transparent repentance (confessing the sin, laying your life back on the altar, and giving Christ full control again) as you deal with this area and other areas that the Lord may reveal this week. As we live the Spirit-controlled life and demonstrate godly love toward our spouse, our marriage will shine as a beacon to a searching world.

Lesson 4
"The Priority of Your Marriage"

Reading: chapter 17.

Spending Time with God

Take a prayer tour of your house. In each room, do two things:

1. Thank God for good times in that room with your husband (i.e. kitchen: laughter around the table).

2. Pray over a conflict or problem in your relationship found in that room (i.e. conflict over who cleans up after each meal).

Evaluating My Views

To take steps to protect our marriages and to close the doors on opportunity for infidelity, we must first keep our relationship with God a priority. Second, we must make our relationship with our husband the priority it should be. Answer these "priority" questions by ranking them from 1 to 10 in the order of their importance to you during an average week. (Don't rank them according to how they *should* be, but according to how they really are now.)

_____ Watching my favorite TV show   _____ Reading a page-turning novel

_____ Having a serious talk with my   _____ Having a romantic date
husband about finances   with my husband

_____ Attending a parent-teacher   _____ Preparing for a Bible study
conference   group or Sunday school class

_____ Exercising   _____ Shopping

_____ Having a Quiet Time   _____ Cleaning my house

These activities all have an important place in our lives. But sometimes we fail to consciously decide what place of priority each should have. Consequently, we let less important activities crowd out the essential ones.

Finding God's Perspective

1. How can Psalm 103:15,16 and 90:12 help us gain God's perspective on our life?

2. What is God's perspective on the importance of guarding and caring for our marriage (Ephesians 5:31–33; Song of Solomon 2:1–6)?

3. What is the first step to guarding our marriage (Proverbs 3:5–7; Joshua 23:8)?

4. Then what action does Nehemiah show us about being proactive in dealing with temptation (Nehemiah 13:15–21)?

5. What does James 4:17 tell us about a woman who chooses to disregard the importance of re-establishing and guarding the purity of her marriage, whether emotionally or physically?

Checking My Heart

Now go through the list on the previous page once again and rank these items according to what you believe God would want them to be for your life.

Allowing God to Transform Me

Ask God to help you and your husband rearrange your priorities so that you begin to build walls of protection around your marriage and close the door on opportunities for sin. Purpose to talk with your husband immediately, demonstrating your obedience to God.

Lesson 5
"Caring For Your Marriage"

Reading: Review chapter 17.

Spending Time with God

While England received a pounding during World War II, Winston Churchill rallied his country with a rousing call to persevere. For them, there could be only one option: "Victory at all costs, victory in spite of all terror, victory however long and hard the road may be; for without victory there is no survival."[2] The same holds true for us as believers. In Christ we *can* be victorious, no matter how hard and long the battles may be—including the constant assaults on our marriages.

Are you feeling weary from the battle of building a strong marriage? Memorize or place Romans 8:37 in a conspicuous spot: *"But in all these things we overwhelmingly conquer through Him who loved us."* Continually recall this verse to help you remain strong and faithful. Thank the Lord that in our weaknesses, *He* is strong (2 Corinthians 12:9).

Evaluating My Views

Chapter 17 talks about recognizing our needs, because the one who meets our needs is the one with whom we will fall in love. Meeting needs in a marriage works both ways. We must be willing to see and meet our husband's needs as well as desiring him to meet some of ours. Recognizing our needs is not an excuse for selfishness because selfishness *always* has a victim. Someone always pays the price when our focus rests upon ourselves. Others cannot possibly meet all our needs. They weren't meant to! Yet as long as we focus solely on our needs, we will always be taking from others instead of giving—our husbands included. Only as we humble ourselves, yield our lives to Christ, and trust *God* to meet our needs can we minister and give to others as He calls us to do.

Take a few minutes to assess your "need" attitude:

• Do I desire to give as well as to receive?

• Am I seeking to minister to my husband, or just trying to get what I want out of the relationship?

• In what ways can I discover and minister to my husband's needs?

Finding God's Perspective

Charles Swindoll writes: "Our ultimate goal, our highest calling in life is to glorify God—not to be happy. Let that sink in! Glorifying Him is our greatest pursuit. Not to get our way. Not to be comfortable. Not to find fulfillment. Not even to be loved or to be appreciated or to be taken care of. Now these are important, but they are not primary. As I glorify Him, He sees to it that other essential needs are met . . . or my need for them diminishes. Believe me, this concept will change your entire perspective on yourself, your life, and your marriage."[3]

Since glorifying God is to be your greatest pursuit, one of the main ways to do so is by protecting your marriage so that it brings honor to Him. Chapter 17 gives seven ways to protect your marriage. How are you doing in each? Give an example of how you can strengthen each area:

1. Identifying my unmet needs (Song of Solomon 6:3).

2. Spending exclusive time with my husband (Song of Solomon 7:10).

3. Caring about my appearance (Song of Solomon 2:14).

4. Laughing together (Philippians 4:4).

5. Acting like a duck (Philippians 4:6,7).

6. Harboring no unresolved anger against my husband (Ephesians 4:26,27).

7. Praying together with my husband (Matthew 18:20).

Checking My Heart

The following questions are meant to help you identify areas of concern in your marriage. Write out your answers:

1. Are my children more important to me than my husband and our marriage? How can I make my husband and our relationship the priority God desires?

2. Are there issues so deep in our marriage that we need to seek professional counseling before disaster strikes? What are they? What steps do we need to take now so we can begin to resolve these and protect our marriage?

3. What relationships and activities do I have with other men in which I find fulfillment? How can these interfere with my husband exclusively being my best friend and companion? What could be the result?

4. In the seven areas of protecting our marriage listed above in "Finding God's Perspective," which ones do I need to focus on improving? What do I need to do to encourage those changes?

Allowing God to Transform Me

Ask God to give you the strength and wisdom to follow through with the action points written above. Begin now to take the necessary steps to make your husband the priority he should be in your life, thereby building the first wall of protection around your marriage.

Note: If you will *not* be meeting with a discussion group or with another person to go through the Discussion Guide, please turn now to page 133 and go through the questions and new material for Week Six as if it were another daily lesson. You won't want to miss the additional insights found there!

Personal Study
Week Seven
Establishing Accountability
and Protective Walls

Lesson 1
"Accountability to God and to My Husband"

Reading: chapter 18

Spending Time with God

We have talked about our desperate need for the Lord every day—that we have no good besides Him and can accomplish nothing of eternal value apart from Him. Nothing can take the place of yielding our lives daily to God's will. And God also tells us that we need one another to help us in a steadfast walk with Christ.

As you prepare to focus on accountability issues in these next few lessons, start by renewing your commitment and accountability to God. Read these verses and pray them back to God for your own life:

> Deuteronomy 10:20,21 – *"You shall fear the Lord your God; you shall serve Him and cling to Him, and you shall swear by His name. He is your praise and He is your God, who has done these great and awesome things for you which your eyes have seen."*

> Jeremiah 24:7 – *"I will give them a heart to know Me, for I am the Lord; and they will be My people, and I will be their God, for they will return to Me with their whole heart."*

Evaluating My Views

To walk faithfully and consistently with the Lord, we must admit that there is no way we can do so on our own. We need Christ's Spirit to work through us, and we need the body of Christ as well. As Chinese pastor Brother Yun said, "It is not great men who change the world, but weak men in the hands of a great God."[1]

Ask yourself:

1. In what ways am I weak and vulnerable to the enemy's temptations?

2. What areas of my life do I try to hide from God? From my husband?

3. What would need to happen for me to be completely honest with my husband?

Finding God's Perspective

1. According to 1 Samuel 16:7 and Matthew 10:26, why is it so essential to be truthful with God?

2. What are the results of being honest with God (Psalm 24:3–5)?

Many women fear that honesty will destroy their marital relationship. But what's *really* frightening is to think that a marriage foundation rests upon secrets and lies. As long as secrets and lies lurk within a marriage, an invisible wall separates the spouses from the intimacy God designed for them to have within their marriage.

Dr. Willard Harley writes: "I believe that honesty is so essential to the success of marriage, that hiding past infidelity makes a marriage dishonest, preventing emotional closeness and intimacy. It isn't honesty that causes the pain; it's the affair. Honesty is simply revealing truth to the victim . . . It's patronizing to think that a spouse cannot bear to hear the truth. Anyone who assumes that their spouse cannot handle truth is being incredibly disrespectful, manipulative, and in the final analysis, dangerous. How little you must think of your spouse when you try to protect him or her from the truth."[2]

Of course the initial shock of learning about a partner's past failure(s) is very painful. But few divorces actually occur because of such honesty. Rather, honesty becomes the groundwork upon which the marriage is rebuilt. This honors God, and allows the relationship to finally grow to a depth never previously experienced.

3. What does God say He desires in all our relationships, of which our marriage is the *most* important (Ephesians 4:24,25)?

Checking My Heart

1. How much exclusive time have you begun to spend with your husband each week?

2. How will implementing the No Secrets Policy with your husband change your marriage?

3. In which area of your marriage will it be the most difficult to re-establish honesty?

Remember, the No Secrets Policy does not mean sharing every thought that pops into your head. For instance, saying to your husband something like, "Honey, I have to be honest; what used to be your chest now seems to be resting around your waist" is not honesty—that's cruelty said without the love of Christ. The No Secrets Policy relates to any area in *your* life that affects your relationship with your husband.

Allowing God to Transform Me

Pray that God will bury the truth of Psalm 32:2 in your heart: *"Blessed is the man. . . in whose spirit is no deceit"* (NIV). Ask God to give you the strength to establish the No Secrets Policy with your husband. This is one of the strongest walls you can build around your marriage. It works!

Lesson 2
"Accountability with Mature Christian Women"

Reading: Review chapter 18 from the section titled "Accountability with Mature Christian Women" to the end of the chapter.

Spending Time with God

God wrote about the prideful, stubborn Israelites: *"They would not accept my counsel, they spurned all my reproof. So they shall eat of the fruit of their own way and be satiated with their own devices. For the waywardness of the naïve will kill them, and the complacency of fools will destroy them. But he who listens to me shall live securely and will be at ease from the dread of evil"* (Proverbs 1:30–33).

Ask God to reveal areas in your life where you are resistant to listening to God, your husband, or others.

Evaluating My Views

An article in the *Worldwide Challenge* magazine says, "We need people to help us walk by faith. If Satan can isolate us from the rest of the body, like a wolf singling out a wounded lamb, it's easier for him to make the kill."[3]

1. What do you think of the statement: "If there's something in my life I don't want anyone to know, someone *needs* to know"?

2. Name one or two mature Christian women in whom you could confide and turn to for godly wisdom and accountability.

If you don't know anyone who fits the criteria for an accountability partner, ask the Lord to lead you to someone. You could start by asking your Bible study leader or your pastor and his wife to suggest a godly woman in the church.

3. How might pride keep you from setting up accountability with a friend?

Finding God's Perspective

1. What principle does Ecclesiastes 4:9,10 give us about accountability?

2. How does Proverbs 13:20 help us with the kind of accountability partner we should select?

3. Consider the four qualities of accountability:
   • Be teachable—How does Proverbs 5:12–14 motivate you to be teachable?

   • Be vulnerable—How does Psalm 38:9 help you to be vulnerable?

   • Be honest—According to Psalm 51:6, how deeply does God desire honesty to go in our lives?

   • Be dependable—How will God reward the faithful (Psalm 31:23)?

Checking My Heart

1. In which accountability area is honesty the most difficult for you? (Circle one.)

Accountability with God

Accountability with your husband

Accountability with a close friend

2. What mature Christian woman will you immediately call to set up a regular weekly accountability time? (Or who will you immediately seek out to help you find a mature, godly accountability partner?)

3. Write out the specific questions you would like your accountability partner to ask you each week:

Allowing God to Transform Me

Write below the changes that you desire to see in your marriage by having an accountability partner. Ask God to give you the discipline to follow through in making accountability a reality in your life.

Please don't let this day go by without setting up an accountability relationship! If the enemy can keep us from being accountable, he is far more able to keep things in the dark corners of our lives where they can grow and multiply. As Charles Swindoll said in *Living Above the Level of Mediocrity*, "People who really make an impact model accountability."[4] That can be you!

Lesson 3
"Protecting Your Marriage through Daily Time with God"

Reading: chapter 19

Spending Time with God

No stage of life guarantees immunity from falling into sin. Age and spiritual maturity provide no guarantee against infidelity, even if it has never been a struggle in your marriage up to now. Whether young or old, we are always susceptible, and therefore must always guard our lives and our marriages. We are all one step away from making some horrible decision. Therefore, we need to cling to God daily for His protection and strength.

God promised the Israelite people that He would build them a protective wall against their enemies (Psalm 125:2). God is also actively protecting us. He gives us a wonderful picture of His protection in Psalm 91. Read all of Psalm 91 and list the ways God protects us as we cling to Him.

Evaluating My Views

Picture your marriage as being a magnificent castle with a wall around it. That wall protects your marriage castle from the world's desire to destroy it through immoral influences. See if your marriage castle has the protection it needs:

• Do you have breaches in your protective wall? What are they?

• What influences are you allowing into your home that are silently eroding the foundation of your marriage?

• What "good" activities are keeping you from spending time building your relationship with your husband?

• What kind of time are you giving to God and His Word each day so that His Word can teach, reprove, correct, and train you in righteousness (2 Timothy 3:16)?

Finding God's Perspective

In a recent study of Christian leaders—both male and female who had fallen into immorality—one pattern frequently emerged: They resisted examining their lives and confronting the sin that was spreading like a cancerous growth within them. The problem areas in their lives were as diverse as having a proud egotistical nature, to refusing accountability, to resisting authority. But whatever the issue, these fallen leaders had opposed an examination of their lives, and they ended up in adultery.

1. What does Proverbs 16:6 say will keep us from sin?

2. How does coming to God's Word protect our marriage (Galatians 5:16,17; Titus 2:11,12)?

3. Knowing this, why is it so critical that we come to His Word *every day* in order to protect our marriage (Hebrews 3:12,13)?

Checking My Heart

The *most* important protection you can give your marriage is to stay broken, humble, and dependent on the Lord. And the only way to do that is to spend daily time with God and time in His Word. Read the following verses and give one specific way you can apply each to building your relationship with your husband:

- Psalm 119:28 – *"My soul weeps because of grief; strengthen me according to Your word."*

- Psalm 119:30 – *"I have chosen the faithful way; I have placed Your ordinances before me."*

- Psalm 119:37 – *"Turn my eyes away from worthless things; preserve my life according to your word"* (NIV).

- Psalm 119:54 – *"Your decrees are the theme of my song wherever I lodge"* (NIV).

Allowing God to Transform Me

As we stay in a right relationship with God, we will also make right decisions related to our marriage. But it all begins with our dependence on the Lord. Ask God to help you put into practice the truths you learned from Psalm 119 above. As you go about your day, practice these precepts. If you are having difficulty in an area, stop right then and read the verse addressing the problem. Then ask God to keep you faithful in applying His Word to your life.

Lesson 4
"Protecting Your Marriage: Other Men and the Workplace"

Reading: Review in chapter 19 the sections titled "Protecting Your Marriage by Safeguarding Your Relationships with Other Men" and "Protecting Your Marriage through Boundaries in the Workplace."

Spending Time with God

Read the story in 2 Samuel 11:1–12:14 of how David became entangled in adultery. Then ask God to show you ways that you may be opening the door for temptation without even realizing you are doing so.

Evaluating My Views

Go back through 2 Samuel 11:1–4 and write all the steps that David took before he actually committed the act of adultery. Notice how the temptation turned into a process of one sin leading to another and another.

Do you find yourself in a process of decisions leading toward sin? If so, how can you stop the progression to sin?

Remember, *"Whatever is not from faith is sin"* (Romans 14:23).

Finding God's Perspective

Psalm 51 is David's lament after his sin with Bathsheba. Read Psalm 51 and answer the questions:

1. At whom does David say his sin is directed (verse 4)?

100

2. Who is the only one who can cleanse David from his sin (verses 7–10)?

3. What does God desire the most from us to guard us from giving in to sin (verse 16,17)?

Checking My Heart

Psalm 119:9 instructs us, *"How can a young man keep his way pure? By keeping it according to Your word."* God's words and wisdom guide us into maintaining integrity and purity in every facet of every relationship. Yet if we are not careful, a friendship or a working relationship with another man can easily grow beyond the boundaries God intended. That is why we must *predetermine* our actions in all our relationships. In chapter 19 of the book, we looked at two important ways to protect our marriage:

• Safeguarding our relationships with other men
• Building boundaries in the workplace

Which of the ideas in those two sections of chapter 19 do you need to implement in your own life? (Feel free to refer back to the book.) Write these down, along with the specific steps you will take to carry out these safeguards:

Ideas I Need To Implement	How I Will Do So

Allowing God to Transform Me

The key to protecting your marriage is to remain instantly sensitive and obedient to the Holy Spirit. God's Spirit within us will give us warning signals, but if we choose to ignore them, our heart quickly becomes insensitive to His flashing red lights. Begin implementing the safeguards He has shown you above. Ask Him to make you sensitive to other ways you may be allowing a breach in your "invisible wall" toward other men. As you choose to obey Him immediately, you will marvel at your increasing sensitivity toward His Spirit.

Lesson 5
"Protecting Your Marriage through What You Wear, See, Hear, and Do"

Reading: Review chapter 19 from the section entitled "Protecting Your Marriage through Discretion in Clothing" to the end of the chapter

Spending Time with God

King Asa began his reign of Judah well. Yet like David, Solomon, and many others in Scripture, he became an example of caving in to sin in his later years (2 Chronicles 14–16). God gave us these examples as warnings for our own lives. *"Now these things happened to them as an example, and they were written for our instruction"* (1 Corinthians 10:11). We can crumble just as easily in the face of temptation. Pray through Psalm 51:10, asking God to help you purify your mind and actions as you go through this lesson: *"Create in me a clean heart, O God, and renew a steadfast spirit within me."*

Evaluating My Views

Consider each of the following areas. Are you using any of them inappropriately? Are they influencing you away from marital faithfulness in any way? How? Write down your answers beside each area:

What I wear—

What I see—

What I hear—

What I do on the Internet—

Finding God's Perspective

1. What is God's perspective on the way we are to dress (1 Timothy 2:9,10)?

2. What can we do when we are tempted visually by something (Psalm 16:8)?

3. What warning do we find in Psalm 81:11,12 about what can happen when we listen to that which hardens our heart toward God?

4. How does purity apply to our "private" use of the Internet (Psalm 139:3)?

Checking My Heart

Check the areas that need strengthening in order to protect your marriage:

☐ Are you practicing safeguards in all your relationships with other men by:
Including your husband's name in all conversations?
Having your husband meet the other men in your life?
Getting to know the other wives?
Practicing the "invisible wall"?
Avoiding/ending all private and personal conversations with other men?
Never giving another man a "signal" that you find him interesting?
Avoiding hugging, kissing, and dancing with another man?
Practicing the No Secrets Policy with your husband when you feel drawn toward another man?
☐ Are you dressing and acting with *"purity and reverence,"* adorning yourself *"with proper clothing, modestly and discreetly"*?
☐ Are you guarding your eyes and ears against anything God considers vile and impure, as well as anything that entices your mind toward romantic fantasies outside the bounds of your marriage?
☐ Are you sharing things by e-mail or in a chat room with another man that you are not sharing with your husband? Are you allowing someone to provide emotional fulfillment over the Internet that should be coming from your husband?

Allowing God to Transform Me

Ask God to help you carry out each of the areas you marked above. If you have not yet begun to implement the No Secrets Policy and establish weekly time to spend alone with your husband, now's the time! It would be wise to discuss the above issues with him. As you do so, the walls of protection around your marriage will continue to grow stronger.

Note: If you will *not* be meeting with a discussion group or with another person to go through the Discussion Guide, please turn now to page 136 and go through the questions and new material for Week Seven as if it were another daily lesson. You won't want to miss the additional insights found there!

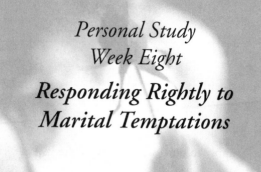

Personal Study
Week Eight
Responding Rightly to
Marital Temptations

Lesson 1
"Feelings, Secrets, the Adrenaline Rush, and Curiosity"

Reading: chapter 20

Spending Time with God

Jesus faced greater temptations than we have ever known. Satan directly challenged Jesus in all the areas where the flesh is susceptible. Read Matthew 4:1–11, and thank God for the example Jesus set in resisting Satan's lies.

Evaluating My Views

We all possess "chinks in our armor" that open up opportunities for infidelity. Yet often we are unaware that these cracks in our walls of defense even exist. Therefore, we need to stay alert to possible dangers in order to avoid giving in when temptation strikes.

Chapter 20 gives us some of the most common temptations that can break down the sacredness of our marriage vows. The following are the first four things mentioned that you should never do when you feel drawn to another man. Consider each carefully, and write down scenarios in your life where you may be vulnerable and could choose to go against the principle mentioned.

1. Don't divulge your feelings.

2. Don't keep secrets.

3. Don't be lured in by the adrenaline rush.

4. Don't give in to curiosity.

Finding God's Perspective

Given the lack of restraint in relationships these days, we may easily find ourselves sharing personally with another man. But those seeds of intimacy can quickly germinate and grow into an improper emotional relationship. That's why we must predetermine our responses to a temptation.

1. What does Psalm 141:3 tell us to do when we sense intimacy developing with another man?

2. Some women may be drawn toward the forbidden by the adrenaline rush of having an exhilarating secret. Others may simply be lured in by curiosity. How can Colossians 3:2,3 help with these temptations?

3. What do you need to do the moment you confront any of these temptations (Proverbs 27:12)?

Checking My Heart

1. In Week 2, we talked about the need to never underestimate the lure of attraction toward another man. What does "never underestimate the power of attraction" mean to you now?

2. How will you extinguish the sparks of attraction if you are struggling with any of these temptations?

3. What boundaries have you preset that will help keep you from sharing personal thoughts and feelings with another man?

Allowing God to Transform Me

One of the most heartening promises for Christians is found in 1 Corinthians 10:13. Memorize this verse, and ask God to help you practice His *"way of escape"* for every temptation. Remember to live from the inside out, practicing the Spirit-controlled life, calling on His power to flee any temptation of attraction toward another man.

Lesson 2
"Flirting, Fantasizing, Rescuing, and Doubting"

Reading: Review chapter 20 from the section titled "Don't Flirt" through "Don't Doubt Scripture or God."

Spending Time with God

As we know, God desires our lives to be holy in every aspect. Living in His holiness protects us and our marriage. Yet we can so easily let "little" areas slip by. Romans 13:14 reminds us of our daily need to *"put on the Lord Jesus Christ, and make no provision for the flesh in regard to its lust."* If you haven't done so yet, "put on Christ" again today, asking Him to reveal any areas in your life that He desires to expose as you go through this lesson.

Evaluating My Views

In Lesson 1 of this Session, you evaluated four areas in which you may be susceptible to certain types of temptations when drawn to another man. Now let's evaluate the last four areas. Write down any scenarios where you may be vulnerable to responding in one of these destructive ways, thereby causing a breach in the wall around your marriage castle.

5. Don't flirt.

6. Don't fantasize.

7. Don't give in to rescue tendencies.

8. Don't doubt Scripture or God.

Finding God's Perspective

If "Flirting 101" were offered for women at a university, the course enrollment would be zero—we women *already* know how! No one needs to tell Susie how to get Johnny's attention. That savvy got built into her genes! Most women so easily and naturally flirt that many Christian women don't even consciously realize how they come across to men. But the men do!

1. What does Proverbs 10:10 say about flirting?

2. Rather than allowing our minds to daydream and fantasize, what should we do (Philippians 4:8)?

Often a woman flirts to get attention and to feed her ego. Feeding the ego is similar to feeding needs of self worth. Both show that we are looking to others to try and feel good about who we are. Those needs can truly be fulfilled only in Christ. He knows our needs, our heart cries, and our yearnings for love and affection. He alone is able to satisfy our deepest longings and to fill our hearts with His love and tender mercies. But if we try and find others to meet our needs of self worth, those desires become an open door for the first kind male who offers us special attention.

3. What does the Lord say about meeting our needs in Isaiah 58:11?

4. According to 2 Corinthians 11:3, what should the focus of our life be?

Checking My Heart

1. Which of the eight improper responses presents the greatest challenge to you in your interaction with other men? (If needed, look back at Lesson 1 to remind yourself of the first four improper responses.)

2. In this particular area, name at least three specific ways you could respond that would please the Lord and fortify the walls of protection around your marriage.

3. Hebrews 2:18 tells us, *"For since He Himself was tempted in that which He has suffered, He is able to come to the aid of those who are tempted."* According to this verse, what is the hope that we have in the midst of all our temptations?

Allowing God to Transform Me

The apostle Peter ends his second letter in the Bible with admonition and encouragement for us all: *"You therefore . . . be on your guard so that you are not carried away by the error of unprincipled men and fall from your own steadfastness, but grow in the grace and knowledge of our Lord and Savior Jesus Christ. To Him be the glory, both now and to the day of eternity. Amen"* (2 Peter 3:17,18).

God alone can strengthen us to walk victoriously. Therefore, we must cling to Him in utter dependence each day. Continue to practice Dying, Adoring, Confessing, and Arming daily so that you will *"grow in the grace and knowledge of our Lord and Savior Jesus Christ."* To Him be all glory!

Lesson 3
"Seven Immediate Steps for Responding to Marital Temptation"

Reading: Review in chapter 20 the section titled "Seven Immediate Steps for Responding to Marital Temptation."

Spending Time with God

Second Peter 2:9 gives us great encouragement: *"The Lord knows how to rescue the godly from temptation."* We can rest in knowing that we have a loving God who is quite able to deliver us from every tempting situation. Thank God for His promise to deliver you from all temptation. Be specific about temptations you face.

Evaluating My Views

Chapter 20 gives us seven immediate steps for responding to marital temptation. These steps are invaluable when your heart suddenly feels drawn to some other man. When you find yourself in such a situation, you must have a plan for getting out! Predetermining what to do can make all the difference between righteousness and disaster.

Think of a situation in your past (or present) when you felt attracted to another man. Go through these seven steps and write how you should have responded in the situation. (If you can't think of a particular situation, then go through the seven steps and write how you would respond if a situation occurred in your life today.)

1. Flee! Get away from the person! (How would you do this?)

2. Pray for God's perspective on infidelity and your marriage. (Write out your prayer.)

3. Resist the devil. (What would you say?)

4. Tell your husband. (Write what you would say.)

5. Tell your accountability partner. (Write out the questions you would want her to ask you.)

6. Replace enticing mental pictures of another man with Scripture. (List a few verses.)

7. Do whatever it takes! (Write anything else you would do.)

Finding God's Perspective

To be transformed more and more into Christ's likeness, we must resist temptation. If we don't, sin will overwhelm our lives and we will not only lose the joy and peace of our Christian walk, but we will also reap the consequences of our actions. The following verses give Scriptural principles of resisting temptation. Write what these verses tell us to do:

1. Proverbs 1:10

2. Proverbs 4:14,15

3. Psalm 86:7

4. Romans 6:12,13

Checking My Heart

Just as we exercise our muscles to maintain their strength, we must practice instant obedience in dealing with temptations so that we will grow more like Christ. And the more we practice, the quicker we become at obeying the Lord.

Remember, every decision bears consequences. By our choices, we either build our homes for the Lord, or we tear them apart with our own hands (Proverbs 14:1). So when any temptation arises toward another man, immediately practice the seven steps above to extinguish those sparks.

What are you willing to do to hold your marriage in highest honor and to keep your marriage bed pure? Write down your plan of action:

Allowing God to Transform Me

Write out these seven steps on a card that you can take with you in your purse. Refer to these steps in times of temptation and practice them immediately. Proverbs 16:17 says, *"The highway of the upright is to depart from evil."* Make fleeing from temptation such a common practice in your life that your path away from sin looks like an eight-lane freeway! Predetermine before God right now that you will do whatever it takes to keep your marriage sacred.

Lesson 4
"Commitment to Protecting Your Marriage"
Reading: Review chapter 20.

Spending Time with God

God is always there to give us His strength in the midst of any temptation. If we try to rely on our own power, we will continually fall. He alone is our Rock and our Deliverer.

Read Psalm 62:5–8 and thank God for providing the strength to persevere.

Evaluating My Views

Read Hebrews 12:1. What does this mean regarding marital temptations? It means realizing your weakness when you are tempted and acknowledging your need to cling desperately to the Lord each and every day, dying on His altar and choosing the Spirit-controlled life. It means starting *now* to care for your marriage, rekindling the tenderness between you and your husband. It means setting up accountability, both with your husband and with another woman. It means immediately practicing the seven steps that extinguish the sparks of attraction toward another man. It means making predetermined decisions about how you'll act around other men. It means practicing integrity in what you wear, see, hear, and in *everything* you do.

1. Name one encumbrance that entangles you and affects your marriage.

2. What is this encumbrance doing to your relationship with your husband?

3. What is the likely outcome if you don't deal with this problem?

Finding God's Perspective

1. As we choose to demonstrate God's holiness and integrity in our lives and marriages, what is the result (Matthew 5:16)?

2. Choosing to walk in obedience and holiness is not always easy. In 1 Peter 5:8-10, what does God tell us can happen as we obey?

3. What is the result of our endurance (James 1:2-4, 2 Corinthians 4:17)?

Checking My Heart

Read 2 Timothy 4:7,8. God's magnificent promises stand before us. Because of this, it is *always* worth the effort to endure and to do whatever it takes to walk in holiness. And such choices *will* protect our marriages! Therefore, please go before God and make the following commitment to resist temptation and remain pure in your marriage relationship:

- I am determined to do whatever it takes to hold my marriage in honor and to keep our marriage bed undefiled.
- I choose not to underestimate the power of attraction to another man, and will immediately practice the seven steps to extinguish any sparks of attraction.
- I have predetermined not to share with another man any feelings I may have toward him.
- I have predetermined not to spend inappropriate or secret time with another man.
- I have predetermined to guard against building intimate, emotional relationships with men other than my husband.
- I have determined to live by the No Secrets Policy with my husband.
- I have asked the Lord to show me any areas that constitute flirting in my manner toward other men, and I am immediately changing my behavior with the strength of Christ.
- I daily practice *"taking every thought captive to the obedience of Christ"* and therefore guard against allowing my mind to fantasize or daydream about time with another man.
- I have predetermined to send all hurting men to another man for counsel and help.
- I have chosen to trust God and His Word regardless of any current questions or doubts I may have.

Signed _____ *Date* _____

Allowing God to Transform Me

If you have not yet made this commitment, then please ask the Lord to make you willing to do *whatever it takes* to guard your marriage. Though a temptation may look enticing, the goal of the Tempter is *always* to steal your peace, your joy, your usefulness, your family, and your life. Giving in to sin is *never, ever* worth it! Predetermining righteousness is worth everything!

Lesson 5
"You Can Make a Difference"

Reading: chapter 21.

Spending Time with God

Picture standing before Christ *"in the presence of His glory blameless with great joy"* (Jude 24), having received what was promised for your faithfulness (Hebrews 10:36). Imagine how satisfied you will feel standing before Jesus knowing that you have obeyed Him in keeping your most important earthly relationship pure. You cannot control your husband's responses—and God will not hold you responsible for his sin—but you can bring your own fleshly nature under the Spirit's control.

Read Matthew 13:43 and 2 Timothy 4:8. Spend a moment giving praise to God. We owe Him everything!

Evaluating My Views

Now that you have completed this course, where do you stand? Take an evaluation by looking at the truths we have studied on the left-hand side, and fill in the right-hand side with your response:

Truth	Is this true in my life? If not, what needs to happen?
I am absolutely committed to abstaining from any form of infidelity (emotional and physical), and to honoring my marriage vows till death do us part.	
I believe that apart from Christ, I have "no good thing" (Psalm 16:2) and can do nothing of eternal value (John 15:5).	
This belief drives me in utter dependence *each day* to lay my life on His altar, to spend time in His Word, time in prayer, and to put on His protective armor.	
I am choosing to live the Spirit-controlled life moment by moment, practicing transparent repentance, and choosing to let the inside (Spirit) dominate the outside (flesh).	
I have restored a clear conscience by asking for forgiveness from anyone alive "that I have ever wronged, offended, or hurt in any way." [1]	

Truth	Is this true in my life? If not, what needs to happen?
I am choosing to obey immediately all that God shows me.	
I am choosing integrity in every aspect of my life, both inside my home and outside, including what I allow to enter my eyes and ears.	
I am growing in practicing godly, sacrificial love toward my husband and others, choosing not to depend upon my feelings.	
I am caring for my marriage by spending exclusive time each week with my husband.	
I have established accountability by committing to the No Secrets Policy with my husband, and also by communicating regularly with a mature Christian woman.	
If I have been involved with another man, I have cut off all contact, told my husband, and set up accountability in order to restore faithfulness.	
I am safeguarding my relationships with all other men by maintaining an "invisible wall" between us and by taking actions so as not to build intimate, emotional relationships with them.	
I have predetermined to practice the seven steps when drawn to another man, and will not share my feelings with him, nor flirt, fantasize, etc.	

Answer the following questions:

1. As a result of this study, my marriage has changed in these ways:

2. My relationship with God has changed in these ways:

3. The most important step(s) I am taking to build and protect my marriage is:

4. Now that I have gone through this study, two other women whose lives and marriages would greatly benefit by going through this study with me are:

Finding God's Perspective

Read Proverbs 18:22, Proverbs 19:14 and Proverbs 31:10,11. Write a thank-you to God for how you are a living example of these verses:

Checking My Heart

Chapter 21 says, "Life is full of peaks and valleys. The daily, hourly choices of making right decisions to climb the hill called 'righteousness' can be difficult. It's often hard to turn away from an enticing temptation. Sometimes it really hurts! But in the end, it's definitely worth the *prize of the upward call of God in Christ Jesus* (Philippians 3:14)."

Are you determined to be the light of Christ in this generation? Ask God to guide you in writing a statement of commitment to Jesus that includes giving Him your time, talents, and marriage. Use this as your mission statement for your future. You *can* make a difference!

Allowing God to Transform Me

As you end this study, determine to follow through on the areas that need change which you identified in "Evaluating My Views." Praise God that He is committed to working wonders in our lives! "*Blessed be the Lord God, the God of Israel, who alone works wonders. And blessed be His glorious name forever; and may the whole earth be filled with His glory. Amen, and Amen*" (Psalm 72:18,19).

To Him be all glory and praise!

Note: If you will *not* be meeting with a discussion group or with another person to go through the Discussion Guide, please turn now to page 139 and go through the questions and new material for Week Eight as if it were another daily lesson. You won't want to miss the additional insights found there!

Discussion Guide

Opening Discussion

Spend a few moments doing introductions. As an icebreaker, have each woman describe one non-intimate, humorous incident in her marriage.

Read aloud these few basic rules that group members should follow:

• All personal information brought up in the group **must be held in strictest confidence** by all other group members.

• When an individual desires to share personal and private matters concerning her husband, the issue of honoring and respecting our spouse is vital—even if the marriage is a difficult one. Therefore, each member should consider talking with her husband and, if possible, receiving his permission beforehand to share such things. Again, this information *must* be kept in strictest confidence within the group. Our goal is to *build* marriages. Sharing outside the group will only bring damage.

• Each person must be affirmed as valuable to God and to the group no matter what has happened in her past.

• All answers to questions and other responses are to be given respect. There are no foolish questions or answers.

• No one is required to share personal information with the group.

Discussion Time

(Note: **Instructions for you as facilitator are in bold type.** Material to say aloud during group time is in regular type. Material included in boxes is extra material to use during the discussion time if you desire.)

1. What do you think is the most difficult problem our society faces in supporting the institution of marriage?

2. How do you think society's views influence married Christian women today?

Throughout the Bible, we find illustrations of how easily we can all fall into temptation and sin, starting with the very first man and woman, going all the way through the book of Revelation. Adam and Eve actually walked and talked with God, experiencing a divine closeness that we can't imagine until heaven, yet they blatantly defied God. And within one generation, their son Cain had descended to committing murder!

Giving in to temptation can happen so easily. How quickly Eve chose to eat the very fruit God had instructed them to resist. How quickly Cain's anger erupted toward His brother and he committed murder. How quickly King David chose to lust, then committed adultery and murder. Apart from God's grace, that same propensity toward sin resides in each of us. If we are not on guard and in prayer every day, desperately seeking Christ to keep us faithful and obedient, it can happen just as quickly to us.

3. Consider Judy's story in the book. What choices did she make that ensnared her in a compromising relationship?

Dennis Rainey, president of FamilyLife ministries, says: "Emotional adultery is unfaithfulness of the heart. It starts when two people of the opposite sex begin talking with each other about intimate struggles, doubts, or feelings. They start sharing their souls in a way that God intended exclusively for the marriage relationship. Emotional adultery is friendship with the opposite sex that goes too far."[1]

4. Why is emotional infidelity so damaging?

Christian author and clinical psychologist Dr. Willard Harley writes: "We are all wired to have an affair. We can all fall in love with someone of the opposite sex if that person meets one of our emotional needs. If you don't think it can happen to you because of your conviction or will-power, you are particularly vulnerable to an affair."[2]

5. How do you respond to Dr. Harley's quote?

6. **Read Mark 10:5–9.** What are the principles of marriage that Jesus gives us?

7. **Have different women read: Hebrews 13:4; Exodus 20:14; and 1 Thessalonians 4:3,7,8.** What do these verses have in common?

8. How does infidelity affect our children?

Living a faithful, godly life in our homes greatly impacts the upcoming generation. The Lord gives us an encouraging illustration of how we as godly wives can have a powerful influence on our children. In 2 Timothy, Paul gives us a peek through the window of Timothy's home.

Timothy's father was most likely an unbeliever, yet Timothy learned Old Testament Scriptures and possessed a sincere faith from his childhood. Where did this come from? Mom and Grandma! Timothy's mother and grandmother were believers, and they saw to his spiritual instruction (2 Timothy 1:5; 3:14,15). Since the vast majority of believers come to Christ before the age of eighteen, mothers have a significant role to play in the next generation's spiritual heritage!

9. Why is a marriage worth saving even if the wife hasn't been faithful to her husband?

Astronaut Charlie Duke flew to the moon, yet his marriage was sinking below ground. "'Our story really is the power of God to heal relationships,' Charlie says. 'I don't care how broken a relationship is; Jesus can heal it if we are humble and seek God's will. It's been a tremendously exciting adventure as we walk with the Lord as a couple and see God's hand in our marriage as He saved us from the divorce court.'"[3]

The Bible considers marriage as a covenant or a life-long pledge. Kay Coles James, director of the U.S. Office of Personnel Management, says, "After I realized marriage meant forever, my marriage flourished. Forever is not a ball and chain; it is a concept that enables us to truly enjoy the freedom of commitment. It is the cornerstone of marriage."[4]

10. Why is it so important that we consider our marriage vows as permanent?

From God's perspective, our marriages are a symbol to the world of Christ's relationship with His bride, which is the church. Therefore, He requires us to guard and protect our marriages, not only for our own sakes, but also for a watching world.

Prayer Time

Each week, the group will spend time praying for one another. This week, pray for each other's marriage relationships.

Allow group members to mention their prayer requests. Then ask for volunteers to pray for each request. Encourage group members to keep a list of prayer concerns in their workbook so that they can pray for each other between sessions. However, in recording anything personal use the person's initials or no name at all to protect their privacy.

Discussion Guide
Week Two Conversation

Opening Discussion

Give each woman a slip of paper and make sure everyone has a pencil. Print this sentence on your slip of paper without showing anyone what you write:

The cook makes a big dish in time for the noon meal.

Hand your slip of paper to the person beside you. That person copies the sentence onto her slip of paper, but changes one letter. She can drop a letter, add a letter, or substitute a letter, but the new word she creates must be an actual word, and it doesn't have to make sense within the sentence. For example:

The **b**ook makes a big dish in time for the noon meal.
Or
The cook **t**akes a big dish in time for the noon meal.

Then the next person takes the new slip of paper and changes a letter. For example:

The book makes a **p**ig dish in time for the noon meal.
Or
The cook takes a big dish in **l**ime for the noon meal.

The sentence goes around the circle of women until everyone has had a chance to change a letter. Then have someone read the original sentence and the final, altered sentence. The final sentence will have changed meaning or become hilariously nonsensical.

Discuss these questions:

How does this activity help us understand what happens when we do not tell the truth to our husband?

What are some negative consequences of being deceitful in our marriage?

Discussion Time

(Note: **Instructions for you as facilitator are in bold type.** Material to say aloud during group time is in regular type. Material included in boxes is extra material to use during the discussion time if you desire.)

1. Why is it so important that we heed God's call to turn from our sins (repent)?

Like a loving father seeking to protect his children, God offers us the gift of repentance so that we will turn from our sin and the devastation that it brings. But if we continue to ignore God's gracious offer to repent and turn back to Him, our hearts can become so hardened that we no longer desire to leave the sin. And as we've seen, sin only multiplies into greater sin, becoming a ball and chain that we drag with us through life. What freedom we can experience if we will confess and turn from our sin, breaking the chain that held us captive!

2. **Read Ecclesiastes 5:4.** Why is it so essential to regard your wedding vows as sacred before God?

3. **Read Proverbs 12:20.** What is the contrast found in this verse? How does this apply to a person involved in infidelity?

4. Why is it so important to be honest with yourself first? (**Make sure that the issue of rationalization is addressed here. Talk about how the human mind is able to rationalize any sin, whether it is fantasizing, adultery, or murder. However, God is not a God of excuses, and we are held accountable for our choices and our actions.**)

5. **Read Jeremiah 32:27.** How does being honest with God provide the key for changing wrong behavior?

6. What difference will it make in your time with God if you truly believe that the quality of every relationship in your life depends upon your relationship with the Lord?

7. God's design for marriage is that the two become "one flesh." **Have a volunteer read Matthew 19:4-6.** How does becoming "one flesh" in marriage relate to the No Secrets Policy? (**Do not let your group members get hung up on the No Secrets Policy here. It will be discussed in greater detail during Week Seven. For now, keep emphasizing the need for each person to ask the Lord for willingness to do whatever He desires.**)

The spiritual and emotional aspects of being "one flesh" can only fully be realized in a marriage free of secrets and deceit. The No Secrets Policy, of course, must be accomplished sensitively, in a spirit of humble brokenness over our sin. Because this issue is so important for the intimacy, health, and protection of *any* marriage, we will come back to it at a later time. But for now, keep asking the Lord to make you willing to do whatever He calls you to do for the sake of protecting and building your marriage.

8. What steps should a woman take to cut off all contact with a man with whom she has had an improper relationship, whether emotionally or physically:

At work?
In her neighborhood?
At her church?

9. How are you working to build trust in your marriage relationship?

Prayer Time

Use this time to pray for difficulties group members may be having with maintaining honesty and implementing the No Secrets Policy in their marriage. Steer other members away from giving advice, but instead encourage each other and pray for the specific situations mentioned. Remind group members about the need to **keep all discussions confidential**, and to continue praying for one another throughout the week.

Discussion Guide
Week Three Conversation

Opening Discussion

Discuss how the spiritual walk of each marriage partner affects the marriage relationship. Then have group members explain how each of the following contrasting attitudes plays a part in tearing down or building up a marriage:

Pride/humility
Lust/purity
Condemnation/conviction
Unfaithfulness/commitment

Discussion Time

(Note: **Instructions for you as facilitator are in bold type.** Material to say aloud during group time is in regular type. Material included in boxes is extra material to use during the discussion time if you desire.)

1. Why is a personal relationship with Christ so critical to a marriage?

2. Why do you think Satan tries so hard to destroy marriages?

3. In what ways does pride hinder our walk with God? Give examples from your life.

To stay transparent before God, no act of disobedience is too small to confess. As humans, we would tend to think that Adam and Eve's act of eating a piece of forbidden fruit was a pretty minor infraction. But in God's eyes, it was an act of man exerting his will above God's—the consequences of which affected the entire creation! Every act of disobedience reflects the exact same sin as Adam and Eve's—*pride*.

Pride is the root of every sin under the sun. Pride says, "I want *my* way over God's way." Pride doesn't want me to allow God to be God over *my* life. Pride wants to put *me* in control. Pride wants me to live independently of the Lord. Pride also forgets that whatever God has for me is for my good.

Actually, we have *nothing* of which to be proud! Anything good in us comes solely from the grace of the Lord Jesus. Remember, we were slaves to sin before Christ came to live within us (Romans 6:19). It's only through the work of the Holy Spirit who now resides in us that we can choose righteousness in the first place! Paul reminds us, *"What do you have that you did not receive [from the Lord]?"* (1 Corinthians 4:7). And because we are solely a work of God's grace, Paul also says, *"May it never be that I would boast, except in the cross of our Lord Jesus Christ"* (Galatians 6:14). We are truly a work of His grace from beginning to end.

4. What are the two steps of spiritual breathing used to practice transparent repentance?

5. What difference did practicing transparent repentance make in your life this week?

6. What happened as a result of your steps to establish a clear conscience with others this week?

7. Give an example of Satan's condemnation in your life. Give an example of the Holy Spirit's conviction. What is the difference between the two?

8. What does being *"dead to sin but alive to God in Christ Jesus"* (Romans 6:11) look like in your life?

9. **Read each of the verses and then have a volunteer answer the question.** With your new nature in Christ, how are you to respond to:

• Your flesh (Romans 13:14)?[5]

• Your mind (2 Corinthians 10:5)?[6]

• Your words (Ephesians 4:29)?[7]

• Your marriage (Proverbs 31:10–12)?[8]

• Your children (Deuteronomy 4:40)?[9]

• All relationships (Galatians 5:13,14)?[10]

10. How has your perspective on life and on your marriage changed since you laid yourself on the altar before God?

Judy's story: I love bicycling, and one day stands out in particular. Sweat rolled down my face and into my eyes that bright afternoon as I laboriously pumped my bike up a steep incline. Climbing that hill had required months of discipline, training, and perseverance. For a long time, I had wondered if I could ever conquer this particular hill. Now, after a long arduous climb, I had finally reached the peak. However, cruising back down the slope demanded no effort whatsoever.

Living the Spirit-controlled life is like pedaling up that hill. To stay in a right relationship with God and with others requires the constant practice of confession and transparent repentance. To conquer sin and temptation require the constant practice of living from the inside out.

But when we sit back and begin to "cruise" through life, we immediately begin rolling down the hill called "backsliding," hardening our hearts toward God and building walls in our relationships with others. It's very easy to become complacent, like the people in the Laodicean church. The Lord warned them, *"I know your deeds, that you are neither cold nor hot; I would that you were cold or hot. So because you are lukewarm, and neither hot nor cold, I will spit you out of My mouth"* (Revelation 3:15,16). He also warns, *"And I will punish the men who are stagnant in spirit, who say in their hearts, 'The Lord will not do good or evil!'"* (Zephaniah 1:12). Wow! God obviously hates spiritual inertia in a person's life!

Although dying on the altar daily and walking victoriously over sin may be challenging, *"His divine power has granted to us everything pertaining to life and godliness"* (2 Peter 1:3). We don't have to choose to sin anymore!

Prayer Time

It is important for your group members to pray for each other as they grow in their understanding of living the Spirit-controlled life. Divide the group into pairs. Try to pair up each woman with someone she is not as familiar with so that your group will not split into cliques.

Have each partner pray for the other's commitment to lay herself on God's altar. Also, pray specifically for difficult areas she may be experiencing. Encourage the partners to write prayer concerns in their books (with the person's initials only) so that they can remember to pray for one another during the week.

Opening Discussion

Developing a consistent, daily Quiet Time with God is essential for spiritual growth and for building a good marriage. Within your group, discuss what effect having a Bible study and daily Bible reading and prayer time has had on various members' personal spiritual growth over the past several weeks. Encourage members to describe particular situations where having a Quiet Time made a difference.

Discussion Time

(Note: **Instructions for you as facilitator are in bold type.** Material to say aloud during group time is in regular type. Material included in boxes is extra material to use during the discussion time if you desire.)

1. What is the result of taking our tendency to sin lightly and not recognizing our totally fallen nature?

    Proverbs 26:12 warns us about thinking we are okay on our own. **Read the verse.** We desperately need time in God's presence in order to transform us every single day!

2. What is the result of truly believing you have no good apart from Christ's Spirit within you, and that apart from His work through you, you can do nothing of eternal value?

3. What did you learn from the illustrations of Eric Liddell, Stottler, and Esther about being available to God for His purposes at any moment?

> Mary and her sister Martha loved the Lord Jesus, and Mary always hung on His words, remaining spiritually sensitive. She evidently understood and believed Jesus' predictions of His death, because Mary took the one opportunity available to anoint His body for burial by pouring very costly perfume upon Him. She never had another chance to anoint Jesus' body

> because when the women later came to the tomb, it was empty. Jesus highly commended Mary's actions when He said, *"Truly I say to you, wherever this gospel is preached in the whole world, what this woman has done shall also be spoken of in memory of her"* (Matthew 26:13). That was her moment.

4. **Have a volunteer read 2 Corinthians 12:9,10.** According to 2 Corinthians 12:9,10, God uses our weaknesses to His glory. How have you found this to be true in your life?

5. What did you learn about the reliability and trustworthiness of God's Word, even when the world's events seem contradictory?

6. How can treasuring God's Word in your heart (Psalm 119:11) make a difference in your daily life?

Judy writes: If we let it, God's Word truly does convict and transform our lives. Many years ago, jealousy toward my brother Steve consumed my soul. Having allowed jealousy to fester inside me, it produced anger, resentment, and bitterness. One day I read James 3:16: *"Where jealousy and selfish ambition exist, there is disorder and every evil thing."* God's Word pierced my heart and convicted me of this consuming poison I had allowed in my life.

So I decided to see what the Bible taught about jealousy. Using an exhaustive concordance, I listed all the verses containing "jealous" or "jealousy," then wrote them out on a piece of paper. I saw that not only did jealousy produce *"disorder and every evil thing,"* but the real clincher came when I read that the Pharisees crucified Christ *because of jealousy* (Mark 15:10)! The same poisonous attitude in me was what killed my Lord! Then and there I confessed my sin and chose to never again allow that kind of destructive force in my life. Oh, the blessed conviction of God's Word!

7. Why is "Dying" (laying your life on the altar) such an important way to start your time in prayer?

> Judy tells of her experience: How quickly we can crawl off the altar! Sometimes in the middle of the day Stottler will suggest that we pray over a decision, and periodically my internal response is, "I don't *feel* like praying!" Instantly, flashing red warning lights erupt inside me: "Warning! Warning! Brick laying in process!" My response reveals a brick of rebellion within me that doesn't want to be humbled to seek the Lord's will. I would rather make my *own* choices without "interference" from the Almighty. Thus, I have once

again begun construction on a wall of pride and rebellion between me and the Lord.

It's so silly! Why wouldn't I want to pray and seek the One who gives wisdom for every decision? Why wouldn't I eagerly seek God's will, knowing that it always results in what is best for me? So whenever I sense that tiny inner resistance, I again quickly choose to crucify my pride and crawl back up on His altar.

8. What does unconfessed sin do to your intimacy with God?

9. How can wearing the armor of God each day make a difference in your responses to daily temptations?

The beginning of the Ephesians 6 passage says, *"Take up the full armor of God, that you may be able to resist in the evil day"* (v.13). The logical antithesis is that if we don't take up the armor, then we won't be able to resist when temptations come. *"For though we walk in the flesh, we do not war according to the flesh, for the weapons of our warfare are not of the flesh, but divinely powerful for the destruction of fortresses"* (2 Corinthians 10:3,4). God has provided the armor that covers us from head to toe. All we have to do is pick it up, put it on, and walk in it. Then *"the battle is the Lord's"* (1 Samuel 17:47).

10. What does it mean to pray specifically? Give an example from your own life of a specific answer to a specific question you asked God.

Prayer Time

Introduce your group members to praying through Scripture. This means using words and phrases from the Bible that apply to a certain situation as you make your requests to God. The following verses can be used, or group members can also find their own favorites. Have volunteers mention a prayer request and a verse that shows how to pray for that request. Ask someone to pray for the request, using the phrases from the Bible verse in her prayer.

1 Peter 3:15—Asking God to help prepare you for witnessing about your faith.
Galatians 5:16—Obeying God in an area of temptation.
Matthew 19:26—Having hope in a difficult situation.
1 Peter 5:7—Asking God to help you stop worrying and to trust Him instead.
Psalm 51:17—Asking God to help you live in broken humility.

Discussion Guide
Week Five Conversation

Opening Discussion

Bring these materials to your group meeting: 2 clear glasses half full of sugar; a cup of dirt; spoons; powdered drink mixed with water; glasses.

Ask: How important is purity to you? How significant is it when you allow just a little impurity in your life? **Hold up one of the glasses of sugar.** Let's say that this sugar represents our purity. Right now, it's pure. We could use it for many things. Today, we'll use it to sweeten our drinks. **Give everyone a glass and pour each person some unsweetened powdered drink.** The drink you have is unsweetened. I'll pass around the sugar so that you can add as much as you like. But first, I'm going to add an ingredient to the sugar. I'm sure you won't mind. **Spoon in several heaping spoonsful of dirt into the sugar and stir. Hand the sugar glass to the first person in the group.** How do you feel about this sugar now? Do you want any of it in your drink? No, because it has lost its purity. **Bring out the second glass of sugar. Pass it around, allowing people to spoon sugar into their drinks. While they do this, compare the sugar's purity to our purity. Discuss how purity and integrity are related.**

Discussion Time

(Note: **Instructions for you as facilitator are in bold type.** Material to say aloud during group time is in regular type. Material included in boxes is extra material to use during the discussion time if you desire.)

1. What are the three elements of obedience? Share examples from your own life or from the Bible that illustrate each of these three elements.

2. The motivations for obedience are: trust, protection from sin, blessings and rewards, and how it affects others. How do these motivate your own walk with the Lord?

God loves to bless our obedience, and encourages us to seek for the reward. All through the Old Testament, we see that when the Israelites obeyed the Lord, He multiplied their blessings. Because David walked in righteousness and loved the Lord with all his heart, God blessed him with a great kingdom and an eternal lineage. Ruth, Hannah, Esther, and Elizabeth all trusted their lives to the Lord's sovereignty and received wonderful blessings.[11]

On the other hand, God warns us that *"your sins have withheld good from you"* (Jeremiah 5:25). In Joshua chapter 7 we read the story of Achan, a man caught by the lust of his eyes. He disobeyed the Lord and "secretly" took items that God had forbidden. The consequence of his actions cost him and his entire family their lives, as well as thirty-six other men! Disobedience not only affects us, but it's far-reaching effects hurt the lives of so many around us. *No act of disobedience is insignificant!*

3. Give an example of how your obedience or disobedience to God during a difficult situation affected your family's or friends' lives.

4. Discuss your understanding of why living the Spirit-controlled life and having daily time with the Lord are the two most essential elements for your life.

Judy says: Attempting to have daily quiet times without living the Spirit-controlled life surely leads to failure because only the Spirit can transform our actions moment by moment. Equally as disastrous is attempting to live a Spirit-controlled life without daily Quiet Times because we cannot understand God's will without time in His Word. Leading up to my time in the Caribbean, I thought I could live the Spirit-controlled life without having His daily input. But without His Word correcting and training me in righteousness, my heart quickly hardened and I slid into sin.

5. Why is it so important to gauge our behavior against the example of Christ rather than against that of other people?

6. What does this statement mean in your marriage: "Integrity begins at home"?

7. **Read Luke 16:10.** How have you found Luke 16:10 to be true in your life?

It's so much easier to "play Christian" by going to church and speaking "Christianese," rather than living lives of complete holiness. What about the other six days of the week when we speed down the road, exaggerate in conversations, live with pride and anger, pour filth into our minds through the TV, and then wonder why God doesn't bless us? The Israelites tried the same approach. But listen to God's response. **Read Jeremiah 7:9,10.**

God owns our lives 24 hours a day, 365 days a year, and He calls us to holiness and integrity in every facet. He specifically says to *"wash your heart from evil"* (Jeremiah 4:14) and to *"guard, through the Holy Spirit who dwells in us, the treasure which has been entrusted to you"* (2 Timothy 1:14).

8. **Have two volunteers read Matthew 16:24 and Romans 14:7,8.** How do these verses form the foundation for our decisions of integrity and purity?

9. **Read Psalm 101:2–4.** What guidelines on behavior do you find in this Scripture passage?

10. **Have someone read Ephesians 5:3,4.** If we actually practiced Ephesians 5:3,4, what might change in our entertainment choices?

We cannot justify watching movies that contain sexual scenes and impure or suggestive language because we believe the quality plots and overall values in those films overshadow the impurities. God doesn't give us an "exception clause" to His call for purity! He tells us to *"know no evil"* (Psalm 101:4, emphasis added).

11. How has dealing with your area(s) of media temptation made a difference in your walk with the Lord? In your marriage?

Prayer Time

Some of your group members may be struggling with bad habitual media practices or issues of obedience to something God has shown them. Use your prayer time to encourage each other in the battle for purity and complete obedience. Divide into pairs (the same pairs as the other week if possible). If they feel comfortable doing so, have partners share their difficulties in these areas with each other. Have partners pray for each other's spiritual strength to break bad media habits and to obey God in all that He shows them. Encourage pairs to become accountability partners over the next week. Remind them again that all personal information that is shared must be held in the strictest of confidence.

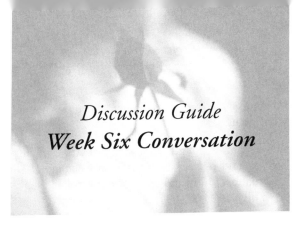

Discussion Guide
Week Six Conversation

Opening Discussion

Discuss how the qualities of God's love should be evident in our marital relationships. Talk about what would change in marriage vows if couples understood the qualities of His love. Then as a group, write a short set of wedding vows that reflect biblical love. (You could divide your members into smaller groups and have each write a set of vows. Then reconvene as a large group and have small groups share their vows with the other women. Remember not to take too long so that you'll have time to complete the discussion questions.)

Discussion Time

(Note: **Instructions for you as facilitator are in bold type.** Material to say aloud during group time is in regular type. Material included in boxes is extra material to use during the discussion time if you desire.)

1. **Read 1 Corinthians 13:4–7.** Which instruction in these verses is the hardest for you to practice in your marriage? Why?

2. Give an example of demonstrating love based on feelings. Then give an example of the effect 1 Corinthians 13 love can have. (The examples can be from your own life or from another woman's marriage who will remain unidentified.)

Feelings come and go. They are incredibly fickle and unreliable. And if we begin to feel "love" toward someone other than our spouse, we can know that those feelings will someday waver as well. As we've seen from God's Word, demonstrating His love has no connection to our feelings. Godly love is one of sacrifice and selflessness, putting others before ourselves. Although it requires constant practice, we *can* demonstrate the godly love of 1 Corinthians 13 toward our spouse, as well as others around us—but only by the strength and work of Christ through us.

3. **Have a volunteer read Philippians 2:3–8.** What do you find in this Scripture passage that you can apply to the way you should relate to your husband?

4. Why is asking and giving forgiveness so hard for us? What are the results of doing so, or not doing so?

5. How do you take negative thoughts captive in a situation where your husband's behavior irks you and he has no intention of changing? (**Emphasize the process of spiritual breathing and the Spirit-controlled life. Use an example from your own life.**)

6. What is the difference between giving up your rights out of love and becoming a door mat in your marriage relationship? (**Emphasize the need to live sacrificially as well as to address issues that are harmful to the marriage relationship.**)

The secret to maintaining the right balance is to do everything for the health of your marriage. When that is your goal, you will be better able to distinguish between what you should give up and the areas in which you should stand firm. Just giving in all the time is not healthy for your marriage. Neither is selfishly hanging onto your rights for the sake of your pride. Ask the Lord for wisdom and seek godly counsel when you face confusion over how to handle some area.

7. How does practicing each of the fruits of the Spirit found in Galatians 5:22,23 make a difference in our home atmosphere, in our children's lives, and in the watching world? (**Go through each fruit separately, giving examples.**)

Because Christ's selfless, sacrificial love is so foreign to anything we see and hear in the world around us, we must depend moment by moment upon Christ to demonstrate His love through us, regardless of what our wildly vacillating emotions cry out for us to do. Those around us desperately need to see His love in action, lived through us, for we are told that His love is what sets us apart. Christ says, *"By this all men will know that you are My disciples, if you have love for one another"* (John 13:35). We don't want Christ's godly love to become the dinosaur of the American church—historical stories with no living examples!

8. Why is the principle found in Nehemiah 13:15–21 about closing the door on opportunities for sin so important for our marriages?

9. What examples did you give to begin caring for your marriage in these areas?
- Identifying my unmet needs (Song of Solomon 6:3).
- Spending exclusive time with my husband (Song of Solomon 7:10).
- Caring about my appearance (Song of Solomon 2:14).
- Laughing together (Philippians 4:4).
- Acting like a duck (Philippians 4:6,7).
- Harboring no unresolved anger against my husband (Ephesians 4:26,27).
- Praying together with my husband (Matthew 18:20).

Judy writes: It's so easy to unconsciously expect our husband to meet all our needs. But when we look to our spouse to fulfill every area of our lives, we invite disaster. If I become increasingly disillusioned with Stottler because he fails to fulfill every part of my life, then I place myself in the vulnerable position of thinking some other man could better meet my needs. For instance, if I subconsciously allow myself to be discontent with Stottler because he continually sings off key and he cannot share my deep love of music, then I suddenly become vulnerable to the next understanding male musician who crosses my path. But if I continually focus on thanking God for all of Stottler's wonderful traits, as well as thanking Him by faith for Stottler's lack of musical ability, then I safeguard my marriage. And I allow *God* to fulfill my musical needs. He created music, and He gave me those abilities. He can certainly fulfill my needs!

10. How are you going to make sure that your relationship with God and then your relationship with your husband are the two highest priorities of your life?

11. What difference might this make in the lives of your children and those close to you?

Prayer Time

Pray through 1 Corinthians 13:4–7 in this way: Read each verse or portion of a verse, then pause to let volunteers offer a prayer for their own marriages that are linked to the concept in that verse.

Discussion Guide
Week Seven Conversation

Opening Discussion

(**Read these two paragraphs to the group.**) The Bible reminds us over and over that temptations will come. None of us is immune. Young believers may fall due to unfamiliarity with God's Word and lack of experience with the Spirit-controlled life. But older, more mature believers are just as vulnerable to falling because we often want to depend on our "spiritual maturity."

Satan never looks at a mature Christian and says, "Wow, her walk with the Lord is so strong that I won't bother trying to tempt her." Hardly! In fact, if anything, the stronger our testimony, the greater the victory for Satan if we fall. We must never assume that we stand above any temptation. *"Therefore let him who thinks he stands take heed that he does not fall"* (1 Corinthians 10:12). And when we realize our capacity to fall into any sin, then we wisely choose to protect ourselves by running in dependence to the Lord and also setting up accountability with others.

Have the group members discuss why accountability is so important in a marriage. If they begin debating the No Secrets Policy, ask them to wait on that discussion until they start into the questions below.

Discussion Time

(Note: **Instructions for you as facilitator are in bold type.** Material to say aloud during group time is in regular type. Material included in boxes is extra material to use during the discussion time if you desire.)

Dr. Willard Harley writes "Either honesty is always right, or you'll always have an excuse for being dishonest."[12]

1. Why is it so hard to be honest with your marriage partner in some areas?

As we talked about earlier, to fully experience God's design of becoming "one flesh" emotionally and spiritually, we must have no lies, secrets, or deceit separating us from our spouse. And if we haven't established the pattern of the No Secrets Policy in our marriage *before* a temptation, it's a given that we won't choose to start once the emotional allure toward another man has gripped our heart! God's Word tells us that He desires *"truth in the innermost being"* (Psalm 51:6). But our fallen nature constantly seeks to find excuses, such as, "Surely God doesn't want me to hurt my husband by telling him about some past indiscretion."

Such excuses won't work before God. For one, if we've been unfaithful, we've *already* hurt our spouse because of our infidelity and the ensuing lies to hide the truth. For another, it's not really our husband we're trying to protect—it's ourselves! And on top of that, if we've been unfaithful once (or more) and have "gotten away with it," we're far more likely to fall again when a desirable temptation lures our heart away.

As we look at the lives of Achan (Joshua 7), Jonah (Jonah 1), and Ananias and Sapphira (Acts 5:1-11), to name a few, we see that God has given us ample illustrations of the consequences of lack of honesty. Therefore, we must obey God and what He calls us to do rather than allow the fear of our mate's response to hinder our obedience. Whatever God calls us to do, He gives us the grace to carry out. Of course, we must *always* share difficult things with the sensitivity of the Lord, speaking from a heart broken over our sin.

2. Which quality of accountability (being teachable, vulnerable, honest, dependable) is the most difficult for you? Why?

3. How does spending time in God's Word help you build walls of protection in your marriage?

4. **Read 2 Samuel 11:1–4.** In these verses, how did David violate the principles of the Spirit-controlled life and accountability taught in *The Enticement of the Forbidden*?

5. What are some practical ways we can safeguard ourselves from getting involved in improper relationships with other men?

6. **Read 1 Timothy 2:9,10.** How does 1 Timothy 2:9,10 apply to women today? Why is this important?

7. What are some practical ways we can guard our eyes and ears?

8. How can e-mails and chat rooms pose a threat to a marriage?

The harm of a secret Internet relationship on a marriage is very real. Secrecy in marriage *always* brings damage. It creates an emotional separation between the couple and builds barriers to overcome. Private Internet conversations deny the spouse the intimacy that should have been theirs. And even if on-line conversations remain platonic and spiritual in nature, when the Internet relationship begins consuming time and energy that should have been given to the marriage, their mates are deprived and the boundary line has been crossed.

Take heed! For a married woman, any long or frequent "conversations" over the Internet with another man create an enormous breach in the wall of protection around your marriage. It becomes far too easy to pour your heart out to this faceless individual in some weak moment.

9. How are you doing on accountability with your husband and with another woman in order to protect your marriage?

I (Judy) cannot overemphasize how the No Secrets Policy acts as one of our greatest forms of marital protection. Please do not treat this lightly or brush it off as too difficult. With one in every three to four married women becoming involved in some form of infidelity, we *must* build fortresses of protection around our marriages!

10. What are some creative and fun ways you can spend more time with your husband?

As we practice building the walls of protection around our marriages, we could become the generation that reduces the statistics of divorce within the church! By God's grace and wisdom, we can do it!

Prayer Time

Ask volunteers to mention areas where their walls of protection are weak. When someone mentions an area, have another group member pray for it right away. Then ask for another volunteer. Continue in this pattern until everyone who wants to has had a chance to give a request and receive prayer. Remind them again that all information and prayer requests are to remain in the strictest of confidence.

Discussion Guide
Week Eight Conversation

Opening Discussion

Use this time to help the women evaluate what they have learned through the Bible study times. Ask what stood out in their lives from the "Evaluating My Views" section in Lesson 5. Then have volunteers share their responses to the question found in Lesson 5: "The most important step(s) I am taking to build and protect my marriage is. . ."

Discussion Time

(Note: **Instructions for you as facilitator are in bold type.** Material to say aloud during group time is in regular type. Material included in boxes is extra material to use during the discussion time if you desire.)

1. After going through this study, what is your attitude now toward the statement: "Never underestimate the power of attraction"?

The eight things we must not do when attracted to another man are:
   1. Don't divulge your feelings.
   2. Don't keep secrets.
   3. Don't be lured in by the adrenaline rush.
   4. Don't give in to curiosity.
   5. Don't flirt.
   6. Don't fantasize.
   7. Don't give in to rescue tendencies.
   8. Don't doubt Scripture or God.

2. Which of these is your weakest area? What will you do to counteract your weakness?

3. What are some scenarios in which you could find yourself vulnerable in these areas? What predetermined boundaries have you set to guard against these situations?

Have you ever dreamed about another man and then considered telling him? Does your heart desire to further a relationship with another man, and you look forward to telling him exciting things that should instead be shared with your husband? Do you wonder what it would be like to sit and chat with some friendly gentleman over coffee? Do you ever say to yourself, "I may be curious about what it's like to spend time with this man, but of course I would never have an affair!"?

The very fact that you are toying with the sin in the first place reveals that your heart actually *does* desire this temptation. And God says that *"the devising of folly is sin"* (Proverbs 24:9). Even to *dwell* on the possibility of sharing such things with another man is to have crossed over from temptation into disobedience and sin. Those predetermined boundaries are so important!

4. The Seven Immediate Steps for Responding to Marital Temptation are crucial for waging spiritual battle. How do you see these seven steps making a critical difference in your victory over sin if drawn toward another man?

Doing "whatever it takes" may mean confronting some difficult choices. One married high-ranking woman in the military has a job that frequently requires her to be separated from her family for long periods of time. Because she continually must live and work in such close contact with brave men in uniform, she repeatedly struggles with attraction to her coworkers. To leave at this point in her career would be to lose all her retirement benefits. But what is it worth to gain prestige and a solid retirement if you've lost your family?

If your job or your position puts you around enticing men who cause you to continually struggle with purity, God says to flee. That may mean quitting a job, changing churches, or moving to another town or state. But if our priorities are right—God, husband, family, job—then the choice is clear. God will honor our sacrifices made for the sake of righteousness and purity. In the perspective of eternity, what can be more important than obeying God and walking in holiness?

5. What principles for resisting temptation did you find in Proverbs 1:10, Proverbs 4:14,15; Psalm 86:7; Romans 6:12,13 (in Lesson 3)? **Read each passage and discuss each separately.**

6. **Have two volunteers read 2 Corinthians 4:17 and 2 Timothy 4:7,8.** What kind of motivation to remain faithful in the battle do you find in these passages?

7. What do the following verses say about a godly wife? **Read each passage and discuss.**
   • Proverbs 18:22
   • Proverbs 19:14
   • Proverbs 31:10,11

8. **Read Proverbs 31:26–30.** How do verses 26–29 describe a godly wife? What contrast do we find in verse 30?

9. What did God lead you to write for a mission statement in Lesson 5? How will your light shine before others so that they will see a changed life, one pointing to the miraculous, transforming work of Jesus Christ?

Prayer Time

Divide your group into prayer partners. Then say: "Whether your husband is a godly man or you struggle in a difficult marriage, God wants to fill your life with faith so that you can experience His fullness and joy. Your decisions make all the difference. If you determine to cling to the Lord, then He can give you His peace and joy no matter what your circumstances may be."

Have prayer partners give every good and every difficult aspect of their marriages to God. Ask Him to work in the challenging areas. Then have partners thank God by faith that He is always in control and that "*the Lord is good to all and His mercies are over all His works*" (Psalm 145:9).

Then have them thank Him for the specific work He has done in their lives these past eight weeks. Thank Him for the work He has yet to do and that He "*who began a good work in you will carry it on to completion until the day of Christ Jesus*" (Philippians 1:6, NIV).

End your prayer time with praise, for "*who is like You, majestic in holiness, awesome in praise, working wonder?*" (Exodus 15:11).

"Holy and awesome is His name" (Psalm 111:9).

Notes

Personal Study, Week 1

1. Dr. Willard F. Harley, Jr., "A Summary of Dr. Harley's Basic Concepts," February 19, 2003, <www.marriagebuilders.com/graphic/mbi3550_summary.html>.
2. Dr. James C. Dobson, *Love Must Be Tough* (Nashville, TN: Thomas Nelson, Inc., 1996), 227. Quoting *Psychology Today*, 1983.
3. Ibid, 156.
4. Susan T. Foh, *Women and the Word of God: A Response to Biblical Feminism* (Phillipsburg, N.J.: Presbyterian and Reformed Publishing Co., 1979), 186. Quoted by Cynthia Heald, *Loving Your Husband*, (Colorado Springs, CO: NavPress, 1989), 61.
5. Mike Mason, *The Mystery of Marriage* (Sisters, OR: Multnomah Books, 1985), 58.
6. Charles Colson, "Marital Safety Nets: Community Marriage Policies," BreakPoint with Charles Colson, commentary #020225, February 25, 2002, February 28, 2002, <www.breakpoint.org>.
7. Christine A. Johnson, Scott M. Stanley, Norval D. Glenn, Paul R. Amato, Steve L. Nock, Howard J. Markman, M. Robin Dion, "Marriage in Oklahoma: 2001 Baseline Statewide Survey on Marriage and Divorce, a Project of the Oklahoma Marriage Initiative," Oklahoma State University Bureau for Social Research, 2001, March 26, 2004, <www.okmarriage.org>, 2.
8. Shirley Glass, "Shattered Vows," *Psychology Today* (July/August, 1998). August 21, 2002, <www.findarticles.com/cf_dls/m1175/n4_v31/20845729/print.jhtml>.
9. Avis Gunther-Rosenberg, "A Marriage Guru Looks at Unfaithful," *Providence Journal* (May 15, 2002): G7, G12.

Personal Study, Week 2

1. See John 10:10; 14:27; Galatians 5:22,23 for extra insight.
2. See Romans 2:4; 2 Timothy 2:24–26; Romans 1:24; Proverbs 29:1; Proverbs 1:28–33; James 5:19,20 for extra insight.
3. Cynthia Heald, *Loving Your Husband* (Colorado Springs, CO: NavPress, 1989), 7.
4. Dr. Joyce Brothers, "Family Secrets: Handle With Care," *Parade Magazine* (September 7, 2003): 4.

Personal Study, Week 3

1. Used with permission from Tim St.Clair, Life Action Ministries, October 2003.
2. "Clear Conscience" pamphlet, Life Action Ministries, January 1, 2000 <www.lifeaction.org/Articles/viewarticle.asp?id=1031103317>.
3. Bill Bright, "Sin On Ice," *Worldwide Challenge* (May/June 2002): 46.
4. *The Wycliffe Bible Commentary*, ed. by Charles F. Pfeiffer, Everett F. Harrison (Chicago: Moody Press, 1981), 1296.
5. C.S. Lewis, *The Joyful Christian* (New York: Macmillan Publishing Company, 1977), 141.

Personal Study, Week 4

1. Used by permission from Warren Wiersbe.
2. Andrew Murray, *With Christ in the School of Prayer* (Old Tappan, N.J.: Fleming H. Revell Co., 1965), 124.

Personal Study, Week 6

1. Dr. Bill Bright, "Insights from Bill Bright, Reflections from the Founder of Campus Crusade for Christ," October 30, 2002, November 11, 2002 <www.crosswalk.com/faith/>.
2. Sir Winston Spenser Churchill, First Statement as Prime Minister, House of Commons, May 13, 1940. Quoted in *Familiar Quotations*, by John Bartlett, 14th edition (Boston, MA: Little, Brown & Co., 1968), 921.
3. Charles R. Swindoll, *Strike the Original Match* (Portland, OR: Multnomah Press, 1980), 165. Quoted by Cynthia Heald, *Loving Your Husband* (Colorado Springs, CO: NavPress, 1989), 107.

Personal Study, Week 7

1. Paul Hattaway, *The Heavenly Man* (London: Monarch Books, 2002), 14.
2. Dr. Willard F. Harley, Jr., "Coping with Infidelity: Part 2, How Should Affairs End?" February 29, 2003, <www.marriagebuilders.com/graphic/mbi5060_qa.html>.
3. Rebecca Valentine, "Amidst the Storm," *Worldwide Challenge* (May/June 2001): 37.
4. Charles R. Swindoll, *Living Above the Level of Mediocrity: A Commitment to Excellence* (Waco, TX: Word Books, 1987), 123.

Personal Study, Week 8

1. "Clear Conscience" pamphlet, Life Action Ministries, January 1, 2000 <www.lifeaction.org/Articles/viewarticles.asp?id=1031103317>.

Discussion Guide

1. Dennis Rainey, *Staying Close* (Dallas, TX: Word Publishing, 1989), 81.
2. Dr. Willard F. Harley, Jr., "Coping with Infidelity: Part 2, How Should Affairs End?" February 29, 2003, <www.marriagebuilders.com/graphic/mbi5060_qa.html>.
3. Tom Neven, "The Work of His Hands," *Focus on the Family* (March 2001): 7.
4. Susan Graham Mathis, "One Amazing Lady: Kay Coles James," *Focus on the Family* (October/November 2003): 5.
5. Also see Romans 6:6,12,13; Romans 8:5–9,12–14; John 6:63; Galatians 2:20; 5:16,17,24,25; 6:7–9; 2 Corinthians 10:3,4; 1 John 2:16,17.
6. Also see Ephesians 4:22–24; Philippians 4:7,8; Romans 12:2; Colossians 3:2; 1 Corinthians 2:16; 2 Corinthians 11:3; Matthew 22:37,38; Psalm 26:2; Proverbs 12:5; Isaiah 26:3; 1 Peter 1:13.
7. Also see Colossians 3:16,17; Psalm 40:3; Proverbs 8:7; 10:32; Matthew 12:34; Luke 6:45.
8. Also see Proverbs 12:4; 19:14; 5:18; Titus 2:3–5; 1 Peter 3:1–6; Ephesians 5:22-33; Colossians 3:18; 1 Corinthians 7:2–5,10-16; Hebrews 13:4; Malachi 2:13-16; Romans 7:2,3; Mark 10:11,12; Matthew 19:3–9.
9. Also see Jeremiah 32:38,39; Psalm 90:16; Acts 2:38,39.
10. Also see Matthew 22:39; John 13:34; 15:17; Romans 12:10; 13:8,10; 1 Corinthians 16:14; Ephesians 5:1,2; Colossians 3:14; 1 Thessalonians 3:12; 4:9; 1 Peter 4:8; 1 John 3:11; 4:7,11.
11. See Ruth; 1 Samuel 1:1,2,11,19,20; Esther; Luke 1:5–25,57–66.
12. Dr. Willard F. Harley, Jr., "A Summary of Dr. Harley's Basic Concepts" <www.marriagebuilders.com/graphic/mbi3550_summary.html>.